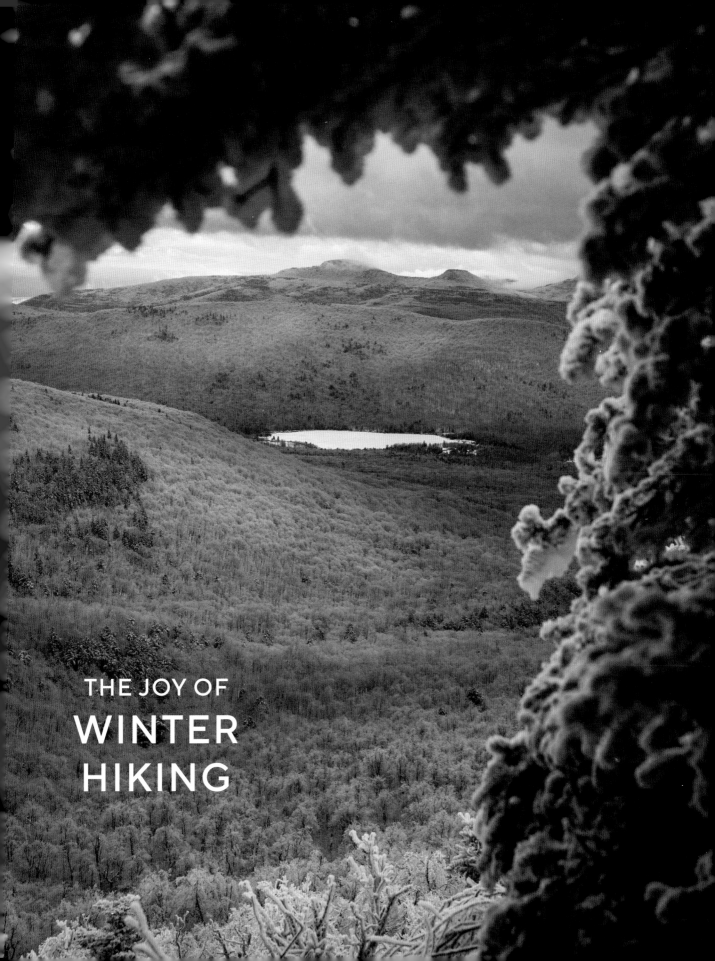

THE JOY OF
WINTER
HIKING

THE JOY OF WINTER HIKING

Inspiration and Guidance for Cold Weather Adventures

DEREK DELLINGER

Countryman Press

An Imprint of W. W. Norton & Company
Celebrating a Century of Independent Publishing

This is a general guide to the pleasures of winter hiking. No book can substitute for professional experience. Outdoor activities in winter come with certain inherent dangers; please exercise common sense, accordingly.

For information about special discounts for bulk purchases, please contact W. W. Norton Special Sales at specialsales@wwnorton.com or 800-233-4830

Manufacturing by Toppan Leefung Pte. Ltd.
Book design by Allison Chi
Production manager: Devon Zahn

Countryman Press
www.countrymanpress.com

An imprint of W. W. Norton & Company, Inc.
500 Fifth Avenue, New York, NY 10110
www.wwnorton.com

978-1-68268-786-4

10 9 8 7 6 5 4 3 2 1

To Todd, Diane, Danielle, Barkley, and Bella.
I couldn't have made these last couple books happen
without all of you—but especially Barkley.

CONTENTS

Yellowstone National Park, Wyoming

Grand Canyon National Park, Arizona

INTRODUCTION

WHY WINTER?

Right now may just be the easiest time in history to enjoy the quiet, patient gifts of nature—while paradoxically being the most challenging time to actually commit to doing so. More and more new distractions fool us daily into believing they are more deserving of our attention than a tranquil, uneventful walk in the outdoors. It has never been safer to venture into the woods—for a human being, at least. Those of us lucky enough to live in a country with well-managed, well-cared-for parks are able to spend time outdoors in a way that few people throughout history could have even imagined.

The access to nature that so many of us enjoy is a tremendous gift. It should—as many have argued over the years—be considered a basic right, a necessity for health and happiness. Time spent in nature has reliably been shown to enhance our physical as well as our mental health. Nature inspires creativity and empathy and reduces depression and anxiety. If there were a pill that could impart all the same benefits that time in nature gives us, it would be considered the most miraculous drug ever devised.

I consider myself incredibly lucky to live near world-class hiking trails in New York's Hudson Valley, and luckier still to enjoy the freedom of exploring these trails on a regular basis. My experiences hiking and meandering in the wild have only made

it increasingly clear to me that there are endless joys to be found in nature, no matter where you are or what time of year it happens to be.

Amid the chaos and uncertainty of the modern world, we have all found our own unique methods to ease stress and battle depression. I am certainly not alone in turning to nature, as I'm sure you yourself picked this book up out of a shared interest in the outdoors. Hiking has been one of the most widely enjoyed hobbies in the world for several decades now, and it seems to grow more and more popular in direct proportion to the frustration we experience as a society. We're so stressed out, we're searching for peace and quiet anywhere we can find it, and the wild delivers. For me, nature has come to be the most dependable therapist. No matter what anxieties may arise, time spent in the woods reliably resets my mood and calms my mind. There is no better antidote to the stress and confusion of modern life. That is a subject that could fill an entire other book, but suffice it to say, every hour of hiking that I'm able to enjoy is vital.

What I'm about to say next may seem controversial at first, but I'm quite happy to stake my claim on it. Not only do I believe that everyone should make more of an effort to get outside in winter for their own benefit, I have come to believe that winter is, in fact, the very best time of year to go on a hike.

For decades of my life, my attention never lingered much on the winter. As a season, winter seems to represent a certain gloominess. Trees are barren and the night feels ever-present. Getting out of work only to be greeted by darkness bothers me as much as it bothers any other sane person.

However controversial my claim about winter hiking may seem to you, I have to suggest that you at least stop and consider this irony. Why is it that we tend to abandon the outdoors during the very portion of the year when our mental health consistently struggles the most?

As a culture, we are simply bad at winter, especially as we grow up. As a kid, one is at least free from certain cultural biases, and therefore children have not yet been informed that they are supposed to despise the winter. Innocent beings that they are, children are left to make the mistake of actually *enjoying* time spent playing around in the snow. As an adult, however, there is little encouragement to participate in the winter season, outside of skiing and snowboarding. So disenfranchised are we from our environment that the biting temperatures and sharp winds are seen as a barrier that cannot be navigated, as if going outside in winter were not simply a challenge, but actually impossible.

In modern culture, you will rarely see anything beyond two basic depictions of winter. First, for most of us, we're told that we should simply embrace the cozy vibes. Light some candles, wear a sweater. Break out the puzzles and whiskey. Whatever you do, just make sure it's as cozy as possible. Then there's the flip side to this portrayal—winter is also allowed to be, like, totally *extreme*. Recently, I happened to stumble across a short film pitched as an ode to the season. Loving winter, as suggested by this film, mostly seems to involve flying in a helicopter to the top of a remote mountain peak and skiing some stupefyingly vertical, absurdly death-defying run across avalanche fields and craggy ravines back down to the valley 10,000 feet below (all while a buddy in that helicopter captures some hella sick footage).

So, there you have it. If you want to love winter and you aren't a huge fan of crossword puzzles, go pull your helicopter out of the garage, strap on your GoPro, and just hit the slopes, man.

Why are we allowed nothing in the middle?

Don't get me wrong, I actually love board games, tea, candles, and that whole vibe. But I don't want to spend four months of my year with only these cozy garnishes to balance my mood. I need fresh air and sunlight. Unfortunately, I haven't yet been able to afford a private helicopter, even after saving up for years.

Most significantly, neither of these scenarios is actually about embracing the season in the first place. One is all about finding cozy vibes inside, which, sure, is great. But it's still a means of avoiding the winter, ultimately. The *extreme* option, on the other hand, is about conquest—tackling nature's

Fresh snow makes for an endlessly dynamic landscape.

challenges through pure drive and adrenaline (and presumably a hefty bank account) and living to tell the tale; crushing a few Red Bulls, washing them down with some Mountain Dew, and living to tell that tale, too.

It doesn't have to be this way.

I fell into winter hiking not because of any specific moment or experience. It wasn't even because of some raw desire to push myself to new extremes. I fear that many casual hikers never pursue hiking in the winter because we still associate the season entirely with the furthest ends of the spectrum, and assume that a comfortable experience on a mountain in the snowy months is unrealistic. But this is of course not actually the case.

Originally, I found myself wandering the frozen, windswept crags of the Hudson Highlands just to get some fresh air, simply to get out. There was no memorable occasion or special circumstance that allowed winter to win me over. It just sort of happened, most likely for a lack of anything better to do, and also perhaps because I'm a stupidly stubborn person. Being that I love hiking, I was bound to figure out how to make it work in the winter sooner or later. Out there in the frozen landscape of the Hudson Valley, I didn't just get a change of scenery before the late-afternoon sunset; I discovered absolute tranquility and beauty in the supposedly barren winter world.

Hiking in winter is far more than a last resort, a desperate method of combating seasonal depression. Hiking in winter is a secret that simply hasn't been spread, a portal to a world of incredible sights and sounds and experiences.

The benefits one gains by building the intuition necessary for winter hiking are so great, that over time, I realized many casual hikers could use a guide that would serve to get them safely out the door,

out into the cold, and back again. Again and again, I've had conversations with other hikers (as well as regular "feeling sun on my face would be nice, occasionally" folk) who expressed frustration that getting outside in the winter was so intimidating, so difficult to confront, they felt they didn't know how to even begin. When it comes to hiking in the cold, our intuition is often all wrong. Any other time of the year, it's no great riddle as to what kind of clothing might be appropriate for a hike. In winter, however, the best strategies are often nearly opposite what the average person might intuitively guess. And the dangers *are* more real—or at least, more easily encountered.

There's no denying that the cold and wind can be both unpleasant and dangerous. It would not be wise of me to recommend a grueling winter hiking expedition to a novice with no preparation. A hiker caught outside in the winter without the right gear may very well find themselves in terrible danger. No one should feel bad for feeling a little apprehensive. Winter really can be intimidating, but its harsh boundaries and unyielding demands make its joys all the more potent. Winter teaches us things that are more difficult to learn during those warmer, easier, more intuitive seasons of the year. Winter guides us toward the benefits of long-term thinking and long-term planning, and these are lessons that all of us can benefit from embracing.

Still, many of the joys of winter hiking are straightforward and even easy, at least once you're out on the trail. The world truly does feel like a different place in fresh snow—or with any snow at all, for that matter. This feels especially true in the mountains. Above any other factor, the tranquility of a quiet snowy trail in winter is something that cannot really be explained; there really is something ethereal and majestic about the winter land-

In winter, the most severe weather conditions also frequently create some of the most beautiful landscape scenes.

scape. It's unlike anything else, and it can only be experienced firsthand. The air feels so clean and crisp; the aroma of conifers lingers longer, and precious reminders of the sun's warmth clarify mundane experience into something profound. These glimpses of winter tranquility are so fleeting, so rarefied, that every time I again find myself in these ideal conditions, I can't help but think: no other moment of hiking could ever hope to match this.

For those of us who are photographically motivated—or simply enjoy a beautiful setting—the scenes of a snowy winter wilderness offer the most dynamic and dramatic landscape possible. Waterfalls become a labyrinth of knots and grooves and columns. Ponds and lakes become strange blank

portals hollowed out from the surrounding landscape, and if one is able to hike through fresh snow, a canopy of pines can seem fuller and more vibrant than any other time of year. The shift in tree cover due to absent leaves also opens up new views that hikers would not be able to glimpse at all during the summer, literally expanding the horizon. And of course, there is the snow itself. Sunrise and sunset glow twice as brightly, and even the simplest path caught in the late-day winter sun can quite easily be transformed into a stunning sight. But as many of us discover as children, the snow does not need any help to be worthy of our attention. Its drifts and slopes and curious patterns are mesmerizing from the start.

However, there's the reason I hear again and again, when I ask hikers why they don't venture outside more in the winter: "It's just too cold," people say. It simply can't be comfortable, most people assume. Cold lingers and grows and seeps into your bones, ensuring every minute outside in the winter is more miserable than the last. Right? Well, no. Ironically, sitting around doing nothing is the surest way to feel cold and uncomfortable in the winter. Hiking in the winter burns calories like almost no other exercise. Regardless how much you care about that sort of thing, this translates to an awful lot of extra warmth. Once you get going on the trail, you'll soon find yourself not merely tolerating the cold, but practically oblivious to it. By the time you've made it a mile up the mountain, you'll be trying to find ways to cool down, not warm up. Can you imagine walking around outside in the winter and feeling absolutely toasty? This energized, invigorated warmth is by far the most common experience I find on a winter hike. Given all this, I have a hard time imagining who winter hiking would *not* appeal to.

The benefits are many—though the obstacles, too, are not slight. Winter requires work. But with the right knowledge, planning, and effort, you may soon feel as if you've added four whole new months to your year. Not only will your experiences be richer and your calendar fuller, but chances are, embracing the winter will allow you to negate some needless unhappiness and anxiety as well. In the midst of a major modern mental health crisis, this may be the single greatest reason I can think of to champion the season. When it comes to winter, why is "giving up" and staying in considered a reasonable option? There is tremendous beauty to be found in nature in all seasons, and in all kinds of weather. In the winter, that beauty will go even further to lift our spirits and inspire us in our daily lives.

In many regions, such as the American southwest, hiking in the winter makes for a better experience than during the hot summer months.

Even a snowless winter landscape can offer unique ethereal beauty

Our modern world and its indulgent lifestyles train us to shun anything that requires such unglamorous effort—though all the while, we are blasted with messages reminding us that we aren't doing enough, aren't efficient enough, aren't consuming enough, aren't happy enough. The contrast of life in the twenty-first century can be a little maddening, to say the least. It's increasingly difficult to ignore the fact that the world has become a quagmire of political, social, and economic turmoil. Yet human beings are able to find such incredible joy and relaxation in nature, we cannot afford to let our connection with the wild world lapse. The benefits of nature can carry us through dark times, and perhaps even more important, can make the good times transcendent. There are hikes that have changed my life, recharging me emotionally, physically, and spiritually, reorienting me to what really matters. And these experiences are available to everyone, everywhere. We need the wild world in our national parks, our city parks, our suburban sprawl, throughout our gardens and our fields. We need all four seasons of the year to remind us why we hold our earth so dear and to let us slow down and appreciate our time here.

Winter offers us the types of lessons we need to learn in order to survive, both as a civilization, and as individuals. It teaches us that we must accept our need to live with nature and within nature, rather than to bulldoze straight through it. Instead of embracing that which feels convenient and fleetingly pleasurable, we would be better off, in the end, if we truly understood how to lean into the rough and tumble reality of existence.

Winter is a master teacher of the virtues of planning, of why we must always think of the long-term as well as the short-term. Winter demands patience. Winter shows us that we sometimes must work to come to terms with unease in order to find something greater. But it shows us, too, that the rewards are worth it. Indulge only in fleeting and shallow whims, and our happiness too will be fleeting. Learn to embrace discomfort, learn to embrace that which may at first be off-putting, and eventually, we will know how to find happiness and stability under any circumstances.

In the mountains, the changing seasons are rarely distinct or clear-cut.

1.

REORIENTING TO THE RHYTHMS OF WINTER

If winter is a long, cold, dark slog of time that must merely be survived, every day quickly begins to feel the same. I've come to believe that hatred and fear of the winter is a self-perpetuating cycle of unhappiness, one that unnecessarily robs a great many people of months of contentment every year. While the shorter, darker, colder days of winter do naturally open the door for seasonal affective disorder, such feelings of unease are by no means inescapable. We begin to view winter as a time when hibernation is the only option—a retreat indoors. But to retreat is to admit defeat.

Resigning yourself to a winter indoors fails to take into account just how lucky we are to enjoy the comforts of the modern world. Winter may have posed a serious threat to our ancestors, who were often at the mercy of fickle weather patterns, clinging to harvesttime and springtime as vitally restorative. But today, equipped with the power of modern adventuring gear, chemical hand-warmers, specialized footwear, and accu-rate weather forecasts, it is absolutely possible to spend hours outside in the snowy winter land-scape without facing a serious risk of frostbite or hypothermia. There certainly are real dangers out there, of course, which is why learning the rhythms of winter is so important when cultivat-ing a love of winter hiking. But when you do master winter's cycles and fluctuations, there is plenty more beauty to behold.

Winter along the Appalachian Trail in western Maine

Renewing Attention Toward Fluctuating Weather

Getting into the habit of monitoring weather conditions and internalizing their significance over an extended period of time is an important habit to develop for winter hiking, whether you're only planning to head out for an easy walk along a simple park path or setting out for an ambitious expedition up a tall snowy mountain. Trail conditions in winter can vary based not only on recent weather events, but on the fluctuations in weather and temperature across the past several weeks. Unlike weather during other seasons of the year, the weather in winter tends to have an accumulative effect. Try to get into the habit of noting the minor changes in temperature, weather, and sunlight every day, tuning in to these small nuances of seasonality that otherwise might fade into mere background noise. While the weather in spring and summer may be limited to only what is occurring on that particular day, in winter, trail conditions will be affected by the changes in weather over the course of days and even weeks, as we'll soon explore in greater detail. Thus, the winter hiker needs to be able to follow weather patterns and read the terrain in order to make predictions. We can gain insight by observing the pace of the snowmelt after a big storm. And we can prepare better by noting that a series of dramatic temperature swings will have triggered multiple freeze-thaw cycles.

Additionally, when you regularly engage with nature in the winter, you'll find yourself developing a new relationship with nature's rhythms. You'll find the depressing sameness of the season begins to break down, and the illusion of monotony and boredom simply goes away. Winter is anything but boring, and once you actually pay attention to it, even its less appealing qualities still offer joy. The very passage of time is a call to celebrate life, growth, and resiliency.

Heeding the Hours

For most of my life, I paid very little mind to exactly when the sun rose and set. Halloween would roll by, Daylight Savings would throw off the clock, and all at once I would become extremely aware of the passage of the sun—because suddenly it was going down maddeningly close to late afternoon. The inverse would be true in the spring, too, these jarring skips finally demanding my attention. Such abrupt shifts always felt painful, in spite of the fact that I obviously knew they were coming. And yet for all of winter, I merely griped about the early darkness, bemoaning the fact that, many days, I basically never saw the sun at all. But what did I do to seek out the light? Was I making any effort to savor the day as it was?

The additional benefit to mental health gained by paying close attention to the timing of sunrise and sunset becomes obvious the moment you start to pay attention. Trapped inside all winter, sprinting from home to car to office and back, one is only aware of the change in lighting conditions from a detached, muted perspective. Pay closer heed, however, and you really do feel a boost from the extra minutes of sunlight, gaining joy with each and every lengthening day.

The winter solstice occurs on December 21 or 22, and marks the shortest day and the longest night of the year. It feels almost wrong that the solstice itself does not coincide with the turnover to a new calendar year, as if that extra week and a half in between

was just padding. But in terms of the rhythms of the calendar, the winter solstice really is the end of one year and the beginning of another. Following the winter solstice, the days begin to grow longer again. At first, this is a slow march, and thus, many of us may not even really notice that it's happening. From the solstice to the end of January, there's no real drastic change, which is why it's helpful to pay close attention. Around the beginning of February, the change becomes far more noticeable—if you're tuned in to it.

As a hiker, you'll notice this shift especially in terms of sunset—or at least, you ought to, otherwise you might not time your hikes very well. Many of our schedules are oriented around the workday, of course, and many people wrap up work at 5 p.m. February is when the sunset begins falling not just a minute or so later than the day before, but later and later, faster and faster. This is because our planet's orbit is elliptical, rather than circular, and the Earth's axis of rotation is not perpendicular to the plane of the orbit. The change in daylight is not linear, in other words, because our orbit around the sun is complicated and, from our perspective, can begin to feel sort of irregular. It *is* regular in the sense that it's predictable and happens the same way year after year, but our brains tend to lose track of such asymmetrical changes unless we're really tuned in to them.

This probably sounds like hair-splitting to some of you, like I'm really desperately trying to savor every extra minute of sunlight using the trickery of math and the slipperiness of our calendar system. Which, sure, is essentially accurate. But it really does make a profound difference to begin to notice these changes on a daily basis. The catharsis of the clock changeover in March, that entire extra hour of daylight we gain all at once—you can have that satisfaction essentially every day, at least starting sometime around February. The extra minutes of daylight really do feel like they're piling up faster and faster. Whereas in January the solstice still seems like it's just behind you, and the days still feel as if they end crushingly early, that first day when I finish a hike around 6 p.m. and can still see the purple glow of dusk over the horizon—that is always an incredible, inspiring day. When the actual sunset begins to creep toward 6 p.m., and I can hike out in fading light all the way to my car—even better. There's no reason to wait for Daylight Savings to roll around to gain that pleasant psychological boost—sunshine is good for both our mental and physical health, and we should be soaking up every ray we can get.

Thus, you'll need to have a firm instinct for the timing of sunset if you're planning to hike in the winter. A winter day can seem to end far more quickly than we might expect, since many of us miss sunset entirely in the winter, and therefore don't have a mental clock ticking away to tell us when darkness will arrive. This is particularly important to keep in mind in the mountains, where the shadowing effects of the summits and deep valleys often cause the trail to fall into darkness half an hour or so before sunset proper. Hiking after sunset always presents new obstacles, but this is especially true in the winter, given how important it is to watch out for ice and unstable patches of snow on the trail.

By building up these instincts, we are not only developing an intuition that will help to keep us safe but cultivating appreciation for the many joys that winter does offer.

Winter's Phases

EARLY WINTER

When exactly does winter truly begin? While seasons may be only concepts, depending what part of the country you live in, they are concepts that can feel decidedly vague (and therefore easy to regard with passive interest) or more undeniable (and thus decidedly more demanding of attention). A resident of Austin or Miami may have little reason to care about the beginning of winter as determined by the calendar. Holiday vacation time and seasonal events will serve as reminder enough of the year's steady progress from season to season. In northern New England, however, or the mountains of Montana, the shift from autumn to the season of snow will usually be drastic and unmistakable.

There are also many regions that land somewhere in the murky middle of seasonality. Where I live here in the Hudson Valley, our winters are becoming milder as the effects of climate change become more aggressive over the years. Late fall and early winter feel intermingled, often for at least a month or two. The sun and skies seem to conspire in rendering this period of the year as dismal and depressing as possible. The days are still getting shorter, and just when the last of the leaves have drifted down from the trees, the sky seems to seize on the lack of color below and renders itself a uniform, blotchy gray for weeks at a time. This period is still technically late fall, and not winter—but I think most people would agree that this period of the year *feels* more like winter than autumn.

In parts of the country that do not receive much snowfall, most or all of winter can feel like this: gray and somber and indefinite. November and

Even the darker days of early winter offer a solemn, stark beauty. With no leaves on the trees and (generally) sparse snow cover, this early period of winter is an excellent time to pay attention to subtle weather patterns, as well as to develop new observational skills, such as tree identification.

December can seem to set the tone, depressing us so thoroughly that we never bother paying attention again until spring arrives. Anyone who lives in a portion of the country that endures these early winter vibes—whether for several weeks or several months—knows how difficult this time of year can be. It's no coincidence that so many northern cultures around the world created holidays based around the winter solstice. In America, we've stacked three of our biggest holidays all within the same short stretch of the year: Thanksgiving, marking our last opportunity to appreciate the melancholy end of fall and savor the bounty of the harvest, followed shortly after by Christmas, the biggest holiday of the year in almost all respects. The doldrums of early winter can be gloomy, weighing on our spirits and our ability to press on through the cold, short days ahead, so we've erected these grand societal celebrations to slingshot us forward into the new year.

For me, this holiday stretch of the year is easily the most difficult to wade through. This portion of the season lacks the unique aspects of deep winter that make a proper snowy day so stunningly vibrant and enjoyable. Without the extremes of deep winter, the atmosphere of those transitional "shoulder" season periods can start to blend into one long stretch of tepid temperatures, mud, and depressingly short days. Nonetheless, even this time of year can still offer great joy, if only we learn how to pay attention. Overcast and cloudy days create a solemn sort of beauty—indeed, as a photographer, a cloudy, moody day makes for a far better photograph than a quintessentially nice blue sky day. Likewise, there is much that can be observed during these overcast days that is difficult to discern during other times of the year. Animal nests, rock structures, and other surprises of the deep woods are far easier to see without dense undergrowth limiting your line of sight. In many ways it is in fact easier to observe and learn about the trees of the forest during this time of the year, after the deciduous trees have shed their leaves. Leaves on the ground are obviously much easier to inspect than leaves a hundred feet up in the air, making early winter an ideal time to practice your observational skills. Early winter is a season best appreciated for its contrasts: the sharp lines of rocks against the muted tones of the forest floor, the dazzling shadows and bright lines of the winter sunset, and the intricate tones of the bark on the trees themselves.

The dreariest days of winter can sometimes feel difficult to get through. What often keeps me going—what makes winter a time I genuinely look forward to each year—are searching out those moments of joy, those images and experiences that, to my constant surprise, I seem to stumble into while enjoying complete isolation.

DEEP WINTER

In the middle of winter, you'll discover that the wilderness expands both literally and metaphorically. Even the most familiar of trails will seem a wholly new place under the cover of a blanket of snow, and the sheer vibrant newness of the transformed landscape is worth the effort of adventure all on its own. Many of the most beautiful scenes I have ever encountered took place on sunny, blue-sky days in deep winter, with not a single other person for miles in any direction. These moments feel as if they're enough to carry us through entire weeks' worth of dreariness, and yet so few of us seem to take advantage of them. A thick-enough

The Vibrancy of Winter (and Lack Thereof)

Winter is far more variable than other seasons. Even in areas where snow is common, the amount of snow you can expect to see will vary between mountains and low-lying areas, and vary as well from month to month and year to year. So it's not surprising that winter often lives up to its bleak reputation but can also transform overnight into a scene of otherworldly beauty. Part of this is, once again, due to light. The shorter days do have benefits. The angle of the sun is lower in the sky, so the muted light of sunrise and sunset is softer than in other months. For those who struggle with waking up early in the morning, like myself, the late sunrise is also a boon.

While we've covered why tracking the sunset across the days helps to cultivate a new sort of attention, it helps that there's really something worth paying attention to here. The vibrant hues of dusk splashed across a snowy landscape make for some of the most stunning landscapes I've ever seen, and in ways that summer simply can't replicate. The "blank canvas" effect that snow has on a landscape allows details and contrasts to pop, both in photos and in person. There is a reason why winter's beauty is so often described as magical.

cover of snow also levels out rough, rocky trails, covers up bramble and scrub, and may even freeze over ponds and lakes (though you'll want to be extra sure about this before sliding out onto the snowy surface of a lake). Vistas tend to be more open without leaves on the trees, meaning that you'll glimpse far more of the horizon than would be possible in the summer months. Even looking downward may open up new sights: with snow packed down on trails and barren trees enabling a clear view through the forest canopy, a glance out across a neighboring mountain or ridge may reveal an entire network of trails that would otherwise be entirely invisible. While the forest itself may appear more barren, winter is nonetheless a wonderful time of year for the observant nature lover. Of course, there's no denying that the expanded winter landscape provides challenges as well as benefits, so it's important to plan ahead in these months.

Later in Chapter 2 we will discuss planning for weather, ice, and more, but it's key that you get familiar with your area in the winter and learn what kind of challenges the snow or cold might present for you off the trail, too. In mountainous areas—from relatively low-elevation mountains like the Appalachians or Catskills to the massive, craggy Rockies—many roads close entirely for the winter. Information regarding such road closures should be easy to locate, either online or with a GPS device. Some roads are maintained but still may not be plowed immediately after a large snowstorm.

Opposite: The frozen landscapes of deep winter can provide some of the most mesmerizing sights you will ever find in nature. Discovering such wonders simply requires preparedness and persistence.

Mohonk Preserve, New York

More commonly, and more difficult to plan around, are instances where small parking areas may not be plowed at all, or may not be plowed for days, even though the roads leading to the trailhead are perfectly clear. The only real way to plan around this issue is to pay attention to conditions when you are in a particular area and note them for future reference. Some hiking areas in heavily managed parks will have their trailhead parking lots plowed immediately, while other, less formal parking areas may require the attention of a mindful neighbor.

The type of vehicle you drive also determines how ambitious you should be. Naturally, those with a high-clearance off-road vehicle will not find their plans ruined by a few inches of snow covering a dirt pull-off in a state forest. Those driving vehicles that do not handle snow as comfortably are probably better off sticking to parks with well-managed parking lots and venturing to more remote trails only several days after the last snow. Monitor the weather forecast not only for your home address, but for the particular area where you plan to hike as well. In some areas, you may even be able to find meteorological information for individual mountains, with dedicated weather forecasts and information such as windspeeds, wind-chill temperature, and the depth of existing snowpack.

Another solution, when hiking in an area with numerous trails but spotty information, is to note other nearby trailheads on your drive. With several options to choose from, there's a good chance you'll be able to salvage the day even if one parking area turns out to be a slushy, icy mess.

LATE WINTER AND WINTER VARIABILITY

By late winter, the days are getting longer, and in many parts of the country, the sky is clearer and bluer. Wild animals are becoming more active, and snow may linger only in the mountains. Depending how much "deep winter" your region sees, late winter thus often represents a more variable third phase of the season, with sporadic days of snow interspersed with spring-like days as well as gloomy, gray days reminiscent of late fall. Or, if you live in an area with a warmer climate and no nearby mountains, this portion of the year may simply represent a gradual warming toward spring after several months of cooler, mild temperatures.

Regardless, trail conditions in late winter are often much more variable than any other time of year. Even when low-lying areas have not seen fresh snow in weeks, hard-packed snow and ice often linger on the trail well into spring. Such trails can often be the most dangerous to traverse. A casual hiker may not spot a slick patch of ice on a late winter trail until after stepping on it and losing their balance. Late winter trails can be frustratingly inconsistent and difficult to predict. Even if the trail appears to be no more than muddy when you set out, if temperatures have been dropping below freezing at night over the past week, or if portions of the trail you're setting out on may be blocked from direct sunlight for part of the day, it's a good idea to bring spikes or some other form of traction gear on your hike. In winter, it's always better to have this gear and not need it than to need it and not have it. While some bits of gear are too heavy to justify carrying along on a casual hike, spikes do not weigh much or take up much space, meaning there's little reason not to pack them.

Even a flat, easy trail can be a challenge to traverse in late winter, when snow has been packed down into hard, slick, persistent ice.

In much of the country, small mammals like squirrels are active even through much of the winter. While we tend to take these animals for granted, they are fascinating and curious creatures to observe.

MUD SEASON

Averaged out across the country, the predominant phenomenon encountered throughout the winter isn't snow, but mud. As the world gets warmer, mud will continue to encroach on those places where snow once reigned, but of course, even regular snowfall serves to feed the inevitable spring mud season. There's no escaping that brown, sloppy earth for much of the year. However closely we may associate the winter with snow, the reality is that only a narrow band of the northern United States enjoys reliable, consistent snow cover throughout the winter months, and this band is moving further north every year.

While the unrelenting shades of brown that dominate winter in some areas are hardly the most flattering accent, there are still plenty of opportunities to savor the season even under these conditions. The forest, while quieter, is still home to plenty of wildlife in early winter, deep winter, and in mud season. Frivolous as it may sound, squirrel-watching is a strangely entertaining pursuit, and one that's likely available almost anywhere. Squirrels are highly active and energetic critters that often move about their world as if performing in their own private Cirque Du Soleil. Even simply trying to get a good, clear photo of a squirrel in the wild is a remarkable challenge. Many other birds and wild animals are easier to spot in winter, as we will cover in more depth in chapter 8.

Seeing the Landscape in a New Light

It's worth noting once more that winter is an excellent time to practice your identification skills—skills that most of us in the modern world are sadly lacking. You'll earn a feeling of great satisfaction from being able to identify even a handful of species of trees common to your area. This knowledge may not always feel useful. Then again, much of what we engage with and consume on a day-to-day basis is neither useful nor good for us. Developing nature identification skills in winter will encourage you to keep up the practice all year round, and in summer and spring, these skills really can bear fruit (literally, in some cases). In the same way that constantly bombarding our brains with curated content manufactured by people with more social clout than ourselves results in a crippled attention span and a desiccated self-image, practicing observation, mindfulness, and simple observational skills can have the opposite effect. At the risk of sounding like a Luddite, I'd bet money that, nine out of ten times, the person wandering the woods looking to identify a few ash or sycamore trees so that they might return and forage mushrooms in the spring is going to be much happier and healthier than the person scouring social media for the latest trends.

For the moment, however, let's not focus too much on identifying particular plants or animals. Let's simply focus on the fact that the act of noticing is a skill we are losing, a practice that we must tend to and cultivate. It is easy for all of us to retreat into our own heads. I myself am extremely prone to getting lost in thought. Even if you cannot fathom why learning the difference between a sugar maple and a sycamore could possibly be worth your time and effort, remember that it's not necessarily about the particular trees, or even the act of identifying

them. The art and practice of identification can just as easily be focused on birds, mushrooms, edible plants, or anything else, since it is ultimately the openness and mindset of noticing that we are trying to cultivate, at least in this context.

Getting into photography is a great way to help nudge you along, and I don't say that simply because I'm a photographer myself. I never set out to be a photographer. Until recently, it was a casual hobby that would pop up every now and then in my life, and I never took it too seriously or gave much thought to the idea that anyone would ever want to pay me for doing it. Today, photography is at least somewhat accessible to essentially everyone, thanks to smartphones becoming the most ubiquitous piece of modern tech since the car. While photography can certainly distract us and warp our minds through social media, it can also help to foster a new way of seeing the world. To be a good photographer, you have no choice but to be at least somewhat mindful of the world around you. Details and timing and daily rhythms matter. The whole art is one of paying attention.

Take sunrise and sunset. Anyone with even a basic awareness of photography probably knows that the "golden hour" makes for ideal lighting conditions. This is especially true when it comes to landscape photography. A small scattering of landscapes look stunning under almost any conditions, thanks to the way that photographs convey scale and depth of field. The Rockies, for instance, will look appropriately dramatic in nearly any photo. The Catskill Mountains of the Hudson Valley, however, are considerably more of a challenge to photograph. Like most mountain ranges on the east coast, the Catskills are very old, and therefore very eroded. In photos, there's very little to convey a sense of contrast and elevation between adjacent peaks, so everything ends up looking like a bunch of low hills hanging out near the horizon. Everything is thoroughly covered in dense forest, too, so there are no craggy exposed summits

for drama. This is not in any way to disparage the Catskills or say that some mountains are inferior to others. Beauty in this context is of course highly subjective, and there are many amazing qualities of the Catskills that cannot be found in the Rockies. In person, the horizon of rolling summits is indeed quite awe-inducing. It feels ancient and gnarled and a little eerie—one senses that the lower, quieter height of these peaks is a bit of a deception, as it can be incredibly easy to get lost in their dark, twisted woods. Despite the fact that it's a challenge to capture the Catskills in photos, I actually love this about the northeast—that it defies the obvious allure of an Instagram post, that its murky beauty and surprising depths require effort and attention. It is an ideal landscape for one trying to cultivate a more open view toward the wild.

A photographer working in such a landscape has to be in tune with the seasons and their rhythms to have any hope of capturing this atmosphere clearly in a photo. Intimate, up-close photos of a rugged Catskills landscape and its vibrant flora are often easier to frame than photos of dramatic vistas. But in either case, golden hour is key. Lighting conditions can make or break any photo, but without an easy and obvious sense of scale to rely on, they matter far more. Having photography in the back of your mind while exploring can really help to build a more intimate relationship with the land as well as the seasons.

Sunset in Bryce Canyon National Park, Utah

In the lower-elevation mountains of the East Coast, more intimate and textured scenes are often those that stand out the most.

2.

BEFORE YOU GO ON YOUR FIRST WINTER HIKE

It is worth stressing that the range of experiences one might have while hiking in winter covers a very, very wide spectrum. Of course, this is true of all outdoor adventures, regardless of the time of year. An urge to "get outside" could result in one taking an easy stroll through a city park—or perhaps one might instead set out for a grueling, dangerous expedition to summit Mount Rainier. When we consider going for a hike in summer, it's usually not difficult to guess which trails will fall within our ability range, simply based on standard metrics like elevation gain and mileage. Trail difficulty ratings often go out the window in the winter months, however, since the obstacles and quirks of a particular trail can vary greatly from week to week and even day to day, depending on ice and snowpack.

Nonetheless, trail reports are common online, and one can usually find a recent trip report for most popular trails (or a nearby trail in the same area) that should give you at least some indication as to what conditions were like a few days prior.

Part of our aim in paying such close attention to the variation within the seasons is to rekindle an appreciation of the finer details—to enrich our lives by examining that which we've been taking for granted. But there is a practical element to all of this as well. Paying closer attention to the rhythm of the days and oscillations in the weather also helps us to better prepare for our outings. Danger is always present, any time of the year, and it should certainly never be trivialized or overlooked when hiking in the winter. A hiker should only tackle a trail they know they can handle—but to know whether you'll be able to handle the conditions of the trail, you'll first have to develop an intuition for what those conditions might be like. So before we get too philosophical, let's address some of the specific concerns you'll need to consider when deciding which trails you should explore first.

Assessing Trail Difficulty in Winter

While this book is not a typical hiking guide, in that we won't be guiding you along any specific individual trails, this is nonetheless a guide to helping you get outside more in the winter. And one of the main challenges to overcome when coaxing new hikers into the world of winter hiking is the inconsistency—or the variety, perhaps we should say—of winter weather and winter terrain. Ascribing a difficulty rating to a hiking trail is already a challenge from the start. Having now written several hiking guides and thus having spent many years researching trails and sorting through the sort of information people seek out, I've noticed that no "easy" to "difficult" rating system can ever really work when it comes to hiking. Ratings will never be tailored to any one individual person, naturally, and every hiker varies in their level of fitness. Even among those who have ample experience hiking, there are some who hike dozens of miles every month, and plenty more who hike per-

haps a handful of moderate trails in a year. Thus, a perfectly average "moderate" hike may register as a mere walk in the park for an experienced hiker, while for someone who has only ever gone on walks around a city park, that same hike may be one of the most challenging physical exertions of their life. And this is still assuming the best of conditions—usually books are rating a trail for the warm-weather months, when conditions are generally fairly obvious.

Winter isn't so predictable.

You should never underestimate hiking in winter. This is not to say that winter hiking is a grave risk to your health, but a simple reminder that it will almost always be more challenging than anticipated. "Easy," "moderate," and "difficult" are nearly useless labels as soon as the snow starts falling. Even for an experienced hiker, covering 2 miles over a flat, bucolic rail trail can be shockingly grueling in a foot of new snow, whether you're clomping along in your standard hiking boots or trying out snowshoes for the first time. And if you are trying out snowshoes for the first time, start on an easy trail, or else you might find yourself tripping and rolling down a snowy mountain at sunset with big flapping paddles on your feet that you just can't seem to get a handle on.

Nonetheless, winter can act as a sort of great equalizer in this way. Snowshoeing is exhausting for just about anyone. The difficulty of any given trail will be skewed not so much based on your personal experience level, but more based on the type of winter conditions that exist on the trail at the time. Many of the intuitions that will help you in assessing trail conditions and difficulty are fairly simple to develop, and we'll work on doing so over the course of this book.

Winter Hiking Preparedness Checklist

Experienced winter hikers consider many different variables when sizing up a winter hike. The most crucial questions can be tackled by running through this checklist:

Winter Hiking Preparedness Checklist

1. How accessible is the trail?
2. How much use does the trail get this time of year?
3. How recently has it snowed?
4. Are you likely to be hiking through fresh, deep snow?
5. Does the trail cross any exposed areas prone to windiness?
6. Does the trail cover terrain that may pose unexpected challenges?
7. What is the weather forecast for the day?
8. Is everyone in your party at a similar experience level?
9. Does everyone in your group know their role?
10. Are all devices charged, and has all gear been double-checked?

1. HOW ACCESSIBLE IS THE TRAIL?

While inaccessible trails can be an issue any time of the year, especially in remote, rugged national forest areas, finding yourself unable to drive down that last stretch of mountain road can obviously stymie a day of hiking before it even begins. Hikers should check online with agency websites and guides to answer the following questions: Is the trailhead located off a road that is unmaintained in winter? If the road to the trailhead is maintained, what condition is the parking area likely to be in? Do you drive a vehicle that is able to handle any snow you may encounter? And, as is common in more extreme mountainous areas (usually out west), will you be driving on roads that require tire chains?

2. HOW MUCH USE DOES THE TRAIL GET THIS TIME OF YEAR?

As with many aspects of winter hiking, the popularity of a trail can pose some interesting paradoxes. A trail that has recently seen fresh snowfall is usually preferable to a trail with very old, packed-down snow. However, truly fresh snow will demand extra effort to break through, so the ideal trail is one that is packed down, but not compressed or weathered into ice. Even fresh snow is not exactly straightforward in its implications, either, as this could mean a shallow dusting offering crunchy, reliable footing, or wet sloppy snow, or even several feet of dense snow.

Obscure, little-known trails are more likely to offer solitude and pristine ground. It's hard to beat the magic of untouched snow and the tranquility of a crisp winter landscape, but a significant amount of fresh snow will also require more effort to push through. Snowshoes or cross-country skis may be required if the ground is covered by more than a few inches of snow. Without snowshoes or skis, you will quickly discover how uncomfortable the phenomenon of sinking into deep snow becomes. Not only is

"postholing," as it's called, unpleasant for you, but it also spoils the trail for those who come along after you. When the holes punched in by your boots later refreeze, the rough, torn-up trail becomes difficult for others to walk on, and is fundamentally less stable as well.

One might be tempted to assume that a trail that has not seen any new snowfall in weeks will be sufficiently broken in and challenge-free. This is not always the case. In mid-winter, or during a consistently cold winter, snow may indeed remain in a pristine state for weeks at a time. In late winter, however, or during a winter with frequent, drastic fluctuations in temperature, the repeated melting and refreezing of snow can transform a soft blanket of powder into hard, treacherous ice. For this reason, expeditions into the mountains in late winter or early spring are often the most challenging, as trail conditions are likely to be more variable and harder to guess at. Regardless, predicting trail-conditions requires not just monitoring the weather, but gauging the traffic patterns of your fellow hikers as well.

3. HOW RECENTLY HAS IT SNOWED?

If temperatures are consistent and there are occasional storms depositing layers of new snow, trail conditions may remain consistent for weeks. Likewise, a sufficient layer of fresh snow can restore the conditions of a packed-down trail. The best snow for hiking is that which has been lightly tread upon, but not abused so much that it has become dense and icy. Packed down snow becomes harder and denser over time, until eventually becoming compressed into ice.

If temperatures are not consistent, however, any blanket of snow will begin to compress and will eventually become harder and sleeker with each freeze-thaw cycle. Such snow, once refrozen, can be quite treacherous to walk upon, since packed snow will almost always turn into ice eventually, and such ice can linger for many weeks. Exactly how dense this ice is and how persistently it remains on the trail will depend largely on temperature and exposure to sunlight. Late in the season, or when a trail has remained frozen but has not seen new snow in weeks, trails may be covered in ice several inches thick, compressed and hard-packed, mixed with mud and slush, and dangerously slick. Such trails require traction devices for safety.

4. ARE YOU LIKELY TO BE HIKING THROUGH FRESH, DEEP SNOW?

By answering the previous two questions, you should now be able to guess whether you'll be "breaking trail," or following an established route. Traveling across fresh snow eats up a tremendous amount of energy, regardless of the method used, and will require significantly more time than if one were simply hiking at a normal pace. If there are more than a few inches of snow on the ground, you'll likely want (or need) to use snowshoes for your trek. Always carry a headlamp with you and be sure to pack extra food, water, and clothing layers in case your hike goes longer than anticipated.

If you're planning to hike more than a few miles and there is a possibility that you may have to break trail, it's not uncommon for a hike to take much longer than expected. In such scenarios, you may get caught by the early winter sunset and find yourself

Opposite, top: Prepare for the possibility that roads in the mountains will be snowy and icy even when the roads near home are perfectly clear. **Bottom:** A moderate layer of fresh snow makes for easy movement on the trail, not to mention a gorgeous, tranquil landscape.

Mammoth Hot Springs in Yellowstone National Park, Wyoming

hiking back to your car in the dark. While hiking out in the dusk or dark in winter is generally not much of an issue, having adequate illumination is a must. Following the trail can already be a challenge in the winter, and doing so in darkness and heavy snow only makes the situation worse.

5. DOES THE TRAIL CROSS ANY EXPOSED AREAS PRONE TO WINDINESS?

We hardly think of wind as a notable obstacle most of the time when we set out for a hike. Unless it's strong enough to blow away your hat, wind usually isn't a major factor on a warm June day. In winter, however, it is one of the most crucial factors in determining how much time you'll be able to spend on a mountain summit, and plays a major role in determining your outfit, your comfort level, and your safety.

6. DOES THE TRAIL COVER TERRAIN THAT MAY POSE UNEXPECTED CHALLENGES?

If you are planning to set out for a new and unknown trail, always scan a detailed terrain map beforehand to try to get a sense for the sort of ground you'll be covering. If possible, look for recent comments on hiking apps and blogs that might point out any unusual or unexpected challenges. Some mountains are prone to persistent ice cover in predictable areas due to the angle of the slope and the amount of sunlight received. Other trails, which may simply be annoyingly steep and rocky in the summer,

might transform into a nearly vertical ice flume in the winter, making them untraversable without the proper gear. Such obstacles are typically only found on higher elevation trails in rugged mountain areas, and should make themselves known with even a small amount of research.

Similarly, if you are planning to hike in an area where avalanches are a possibility, always check beforehand to try to learn what conditions are like on the slope. Avalanches are not a factor in most parts of the country—if you are hiking in a state like North Carolina or even New York, chances are good that avalanches simply do not occur (or are exceedingly rare) where you'll be hiking. Nonetheless, weather anomalies do happen, and this is increasingly true the higher the elevation and the bigger the mountain. If you are hiking in a remote, rugged area, checking in on conditions is always advised before you set out.

7. WHAT IS THE WEATHER FORECAST FOR THE DAY?

Bad weather in winter poses a much greater risk than a passing rain shower in June. If a big snowstorm is expected in the mountains later in the day, you certainly don't want to get caught up in it. Existing snow cover can make it difficult to follow a trail, but heavy falling snow can make trail-finding nearly impossible. Sub-freezing temperatures and whiteout conditions with zero visibility can cause any hike to turn deadly in a very short amount of time. Nor will you want to return from a long, grueling hike only to find your car trapped under a foot of

Opposite, top left: Deep snow that has not been packed down requires a great amount of effort to move through. **Top right:** Summits and cliffs are prone to high winds, which can quickly rob you of warmth under winter conditions. **Bottom:** Rocky areas on mountainsides are prone to icing over during the winter and require traction gear to safely traverse.

Mt. Mansfield, Vermont. Mountains often generate their own weather systems; always look for a forecast specific to the mountain where you'll be hiking. Conditions will often be very different from those of nearby low-lying areas.

snow. Conversely, venturing out into the mountains on a crisp, cold winter day with low humidity and wide-open sunny skies can be one of the most enjoyable, invigorating hiking experiences you'll ever have. I try to take advantage of such days whenever possible, as they are truly a rare treasure in many parts of the country.

8. IS EVERYONE IN YOUR PARTY AT A SIMILAR EXPERIENCE LEVEL?

Because hiking through snow requires so much more exertion than hiking the same terrain in summer, inexperienced hikers may fall behind and become frustrated much more quickly. Honestly evaluate the ability level of each member of your hiking party, and try to gauge how much time the slowest member of your party might realistically need to complete the hike. In deep snow, a hike can easily take two or three times longer than it would in the summer. Be sure to plan accordingly.

9. DOES EVERYONE IN YOUR GROUP KNOW THEIR ROLE?

Assigning each member of your hiking party a "role" for the day probably isn't necessary for most easier hikes, but this can be a good insurance method for longer, more challenging routes, or hikes in more remote areas. Having someone or several people responsible for transportation, navigation, food, emergency supplies, and weather monitoring can help to ensure that nothing is overlooked, and that precautions have been made for various contingencies. This is particularly important when it comes to packing proper clothing and gear. While one member of your group forgetting to pack extra snacks shouldn't cause any major issues, discovering too late that someone did not pack adequate clothing, or forgot to bring their micro-

Forecasting Winter Conditions—A Case Study

Years ago, when I had negligible experience with winter hiking, I made plans to take a friend out for their first winter hike. My friend Evan is a rugged kind of guy, but he doesn't usually go hiking much. Not to worry, I thought—I'd simply bring him to one of my favorite parks, Storm King Mountain, an area that I knew fairly well, as I'd hiked there numerous times over the years. Except, well, I'd only hiked there during summer and fall, never in the midst of winter, and I didn't pause to think about what the topography of the mountain was like. And boy, does Storm King have some topography. Let's see if you can intuit what I did not.

Storm King Mountain towers directly over the Hudson River. It's part of the Hudson Highlands, a chain of low mountains that the river essentially slices in two. In fact, these mountains are considered fjords—the long, narrow inlet of a river where past glacial movement has carved out steep sides or cliffs. While Storm King isn't quite as dramatic as some of the grandest fjords of Norway, nonetheless, the intense ebbs and flows of the Hudson River have carved out a pretty serious set of cliffs on either side of the wide river, with sheer drop-offs like nothing else you'll see on the east coast. Cliffs are one thing, but cliffs that slide straight down into a major river below are another entirely. Only the side of the mountain facing the river has such a steep drop off, however. The rest of the mountain, in terms of trails, is pretty standard stuff. Storm King can be hiked from various directions, and not all routes necessitate looping around the steep cliff-side of the mountain.

Upon arrival, we saw that the mountain appeared to be free of snow. There were no indications that trail conditions might pose any serious challenges. I recalled that only trivial amounts of snow had fallen in recent weeks, and that which had fallen had melted away rather quickly. Besides,

The steep cliffs of Storm King rise up over the Hudson River.

The edges of steep cliffs often transform into frozen waterfalls in the winter.

trace of snow or ice. There wasn't even that much mud. By all appearances, this was simply a dark and moody early winter day—the kind of winter day that can sneak up on you if you aren't thinking things through.

After leaving the summit, we hiked around the shoulder of the mountain, taking the river-facing trail around the steep eastern face of Storm King. This is the side of the mountain that is truly fjord-like, dropping at a very severe grade down to the river below. Light from the low winter sun only strikes this side of the mountain for a brief part of each day. What does reach the eastern face of Storm King, however, is run-off. Though it hadn't snowed prior to our visit, there was still plenty of water to go around. It had rained, and in some areas, water simply seeps out of the ground. At Storm King, any water on the eastern half of the mountain will tend to rush straight down the eastern face. But since that slope is so well shaded, this water is highly prone to freeze. The more ice that collects, the more readily new ice will form, so long as the temperature doesn't rise much about freezing. That was one consideration I had not thought of, at the time: while there hadn't yet been much snow, temperatures had been reliably cold. So there was indeed ice. A lot of ice. In fact, there wasn't so much a trail as there was one long ice flume.

Admittedly, there's something visually spectacular about such a massive, frozen cascade. This wasn't the sort of packed-down, hardened snow-ice you'll find in late winter. This was essentially a mountain-sized frozen waterfall. The runoff from an entire slope caught up in shadowy, frozen descent. Yet for some obtuse reason or another, we decided to press on. This is where our mistake leapt beyond nativity into hubris, foolishness rather than a slight underestimation. We did not have traction devices (see page 80 for my recommendations here). No crampons. No microspikes. Not even hiking poles.

As you can imagine, the going was rough. Every step forward was as deliberate as it was hesitant.

it was fairly early in the season. Not only had it not snowed recently, but winter was still so fresh onto the scene, I didn't think much snow had fallen at all, even at this slightly higher elevation. So what was there to be worried about? We hiked the loop circuit around Storm King and made it to the summit about three quarters of the way through the hike. There, we still had yet to encounter any

Every possible tree trunk and tree branch within reach were called upon for balance. The problem was, the trail there is so steep, any gap between trees represented a nearly un-traversable span of ice. Solid, thick, wet, slick ice. Not the kind you can dig your heel into and find some balance. No, this was all the kind of ice that you simply slide off of, like butter sliding off a hot knife.

Why did we continue on? I truly have no idea. Sheer naivety and stubbornness. Toss in a little stupidity. At first, we weren't sure if the ice would persist for the entirety of the trail. There's always that flicker of hope: "Maybe the trail gets better if we just go a little further." Then, of course, we made it a bit further down the trail, pushed a little more, then just a little more, and soon, it felt pointless to turn around. We'd already gone that far, why not continue to the end?

Before long, we were defaulting almost entirely to that timeless technique for navigating icy surfaces: the butt scoot. This worked for a time, until finally, near the end of our epic journey, we reached a span of trail that had hardly any trees within reach. To either side of the narrow trail was just more ice. Ice everywhere.

I went first, scooting forward, aiming for a tree some ten feet away. I had zero chance of ever making it—my momentum sent me veering sadly off course, and despite my feeble attempts to push forward, I simply slipped like a half-melted pat of butter toward the edge of the trail and over.

Thankfully, as steep as that side of Storm King is, it's not a true cliff. There is a slope, and there are trees. I tumbled off and caught myself on a tree maybe five feet below the edge of the trail. My friend dove out after me, managed to latch on to the tree trunk I myself had been aiming for, and grabbed a hefty fallen branch. Held it out, and helped haul me back up, like the culminating scene in an action movie. Both clinging desperately to the same tree trunk, we pushed off—butt scooting, always butt scooting—and somehow made it to the next tree down the trail.

Granted, this wasn't the sort of cliff where I might have fallen off and plummeted to my death. If I hadn't latched on to a convenient tree on my way over the edge, I might have simply rolled for another twenty or thirty feet and broken a leg or an arm. Not hopeless, but, certainly, *bad*. After all, notice how difficult our passage was without any broken limbs.

Let our foolishness be a lesson: always think through *everything* ahead of time, always carry microspikes, and don't be afraid to simply turn around if you have to.

For more intensive outings, every member of your group should have a responsibility to focus on so that nothing is overlooked.

spikes, can place the entire group into a stressful, potentially dangerous situation.

10. ARE ALL DEVICES CHARGED, AND HAS ALL GEAR BEEN DOUBLE-CHECKED?

Regardless of whether you're hiking in a group or alone, it's crucial to double check your equipment so that you can be confident that not only did you pack everything you'll need, but that your gear and devices will hold up to the day ahead. Most important, perhaps, is that lynchpin of modern life: your cell phone. If you are hiking in an area where you have cell reception, your phone will of course provide a critical lifeline should something go wrong.

While you absolutely don't want to count on calling out for help, it's definitely better to have the option than to not, and cell phones can also come in handy in other ways. Have you underestimated the difficulty of a trail, and found yourself hiking out in the dark? Naturally, your cell phone flashlight will come in very useful. Keep in mind, most batteries drain much more quickly in the cold, and often lose their charge entirely once beyond a certain threshold. You may find that your cell phone battery has suddenly plummeted to 0 and shut off entirely after slipping past a third of a charge. For this reason, you'll always want to pack a headlamp as well. Make sure the batteries of all your electronic devices are fully charged, and store them someplace warm and insulated as best you can. Your phone, for instance, may still be subjected to frigid temps when you keep it in your pants pocket. Whenever possible, store it in a pocket in a layer closer to your body heat.

Further Planning

This checklist is simply a starting point, of course. If conditions on the trail appear more extreme than you anticipated, or you sense a storm is on its way, do not hesitate to turn back. The trail will be there another day—winter is not the time to take risks beyond your comfort and experience level. It really can't be stressed enough: when you're first starting out as a winter hiker, only tackle trails that you're fully confident you'll be able to handle. Stick to hikes that you've done previously, during another season of the year, so that you have a good idea what to expect. Only once you've built up ample experience should you begin to push your comfort zone.

Don't go chasing high peaks (or frozen waterfalls). Stick to the hills and the valleys you're used to!

Ice can be either a dangerous obstacle or a gorgeous addition to the landscape, depending on how prepared you are with the right gear.

Learning how to adjust your clothing and your pace in order to manage your body temperature is perhaps the most important skill when it comes to winter hiking.

3.

WHAT TO WEAR AND WHEN TO WEAR IT

When thinking about how to venture outside in the winter and avoid succumbing to the annoyance—or potential danger—of the cold, it's worth reminding ourselves of two fairly obvious things. You already know these things but keeping them in mind is crucial for developing an intuition for how to dress for a winter hike. First, warm clothing does not create warmth on its own. It only traps the heat generated by our bodies. Secondly, when you are exerting yourself, your body generates more heat than when you're idle or at rest, and this effect scales. If you are performing strenuous exercise, your body generates a *lot* of heat.

It only takes a few minutes of trudging up a steep hill in the winter to notice the result of these two principles, and the massive difference this makes for our body temperature. All actions, whether biological or mechanical, produce some amount of waste heat due to the second law of thermodynamics. The human body is an incredibly efficient resource-management machine, no doubt about it, but it is still beholden to the rules of physics.

When you use your muscles during exercise, only 20 percent of the total energy is used for muscle contraction, while the remaining 80 percent is converted to heat. While this excess waste heat may be convenient—even life-saving—when exercising outside in the winter, it can also create issues if not regulated properly. When simply walking down your driveway to collect the mail in winter, the general practice of throwing on a warm jacket serves just fine. When hiking in the winter, however, this general habit of dressing up in the warmest possible clothing will very often backfire.

The hypothalamus in the brain serves as the body's thermostat. When it receives the message that the body is experiencing excessive heat, the hypothalamus stimulates sweat glands in the skin to begin producing fluid. The heat generated by your muscles during exercise also causes blood vessels in the skin to dilate, which increases blood flow. Your skin is actually the largest organ of your body, and this incredibly large surface area allows excess heat to be dissipated into the surrounding air. And of course, the perspiration produced by our sweat glands evaporates from your skin as well, which also removes heat and cools the body in the process.

With just this basic knowledge, we already have a few significant clues as to how we should prepare and dress for a winter outing. First, consider: how strenuous will this adventure be? Will the level of exertion be constant, or intermittent—in other words, is the trail a steady climb uphill, or a series of ups and downs interspersed with flat stretches? Also ask: how extreme might the conditions be at any point where you may choose (or be forced, due to exhaustion or over-heating) to pause your hike?

If you are planning a walk across a long meandering path through a field that does not change much in elevation at any point, you can reasonably expect that the general environmental conditions around you will not change drastically from the beginning of your walk to the end. As this example walk is not strenuous, and remains consistently non-strenuous throughout, you can expect that you will not be generating as much heat as you would if you were climbing up a mountain. Because you are not going to be exerting yourself

No matter how steep or level the trail, try to maintain a pace that limits how much you'll sweat. Wet clothes in the cold are a danger.

greatly, you'll have a good idea of how cold you'll feel before you even set out. Both your own body temperature and conditions due to terrain should not change dramatically. If you've monitored the weather and planned around daylight hours, you should have a fairly predictable walk ahead of you, and won't need to alter your level of warmth—by which I mean, the clothing you wore to regulate that warmth—all that much. Perhaps you'll unzip your jacket a bit halfway through or pull your gloves off and simply keep your hands in your pocket for a while. In any case, regulating your body temperature on such an outing shouldn't require any drastic alterations in your gear.

Now, let's take a different kind of hike—a far more strenuous trail that heads up a modest nearby hill or low mountain. This mountain is not terribly tall nor rugged, and experiences moderate, variable winter weather, so as a result we're not concerned about any extreme winter challenges. Because the elevation and weather in this area is moderate, snow cover at the summit will likely be deeper than at the base, but not so much so that you won't be able to make a rough prediction. You can see the top of the mountain from your drive out of town, and there's no visible snow at the summit, so for the sake of simplicity with this example, we're only going to focus on temperature regulation, not trail conditions.

In this example, you'll start out your hike in conditions that feel fairly cold—a pretty average winter day. You'll be dressed to keep warm, but you also know that you'll be warming up quickly, so you aren't as bundled up as you could be. Half an hour into the hike, you've already hiked up several hundred feet in elevation, and your body has begun burning calories accordingly. You remove your outer layer. You remain warm, as your body continues to generate excess heat, even though you are stopping to catch your breath every couple of minutes. By the time you reach the summit, however, the temperature has dropped noticeably, and sharp winds are blowing. Plus, you are no longer going to be climbing uphill, and within a few minutes, your body will no longer be producing nearly as much heat. At this point, retaining the warmth you've generated is critical. You'll need to immediately add layers to ensure your temperature does not drop rapidly, but you'll also need to pace your rest periods. Sit still in the snow and wind for too long, and even a few extra layers of insulating clothing may not be enough to stabilize your body temperature.

These examples cover conditions representative of those you'll find on most easy and moderate winter hikes. However, as we've stressed, winter is predictably unpredictable. In order to know how to dress for more variable and extreme hiking conditions, we must first understand exactly how the body loses heat.

Understanding Heat Loss

There are three primary ways that our bodies lose warmth: conduction, radiation, and convection. Conduction is fairly simple: we lose some amount of heat every time our feet (or, hopefully, our boots) touch cold snow, or when we sit down on a snowy boulder to take a breather, or when our hands touch the frigid handle of an ice axe. This heat loss is fairly easy to mitigate, however: we wear warm boots and gloves to provide a thorough buffer between our skin and the cold winter world. When you stop to rest, don't sit down unless you have to. If you do need to sit down on a cold surface, place your backpack under you like a cushion.

The more severe the conditions outside, the more important managing your body temperature becomes.

Radiative heat loss is also fairly simple, as it is merely the constant, steady loss of temperature to the ambient air around us. Here again, the same measures protect us, and sufficient insulation from our clothing ensures that we do not lose heat faster than we generate it. Balance this simple math equation, and you will stay warm.

The third variety of heat loss is perhaps the hardest to plan around for novice winter hikers. Convection is a term we likely know better from our kitchen appliances than recreational safety concerns, but the concept is actually the same. In a convection oven—which have recently been rebranded as "air fryers"—the heating elements are assisted by fans that circulate the hot air more thoroughly. This redistribution of air means that heat is applied more evenly over the item being cooked. Cold air can achieve the same sort of result, of course. A strong mountain wind surging through the openings in your clothing can literally pull warmth away from your body, "redistributing" your heat into the open air, just as a convection oven shifts currents of heat to ensure that your tater tots are extra crispy all over. This effect, however, is much less of a concern when you're dressed in the right clothing, and with proper layering. Snug layers with limited openings will go a long way in keeping you warm, especially with additional protections in the form of windbreakers, adjustable hoods, balaclavas, and other gear with ventilation and snugness considered in the design.

This same principle also explains why you'll usually feel so much more uncomfortable in cold humid air than in cold dry air, even if the dry air is in fact several degrees colder. Most of us are already aware of this concept when it comes to heat—you'll hear it referenced all the time when traveling from the east coast to the west coast. Moist, humid air is simply a more efficient heat transfer medium than dry air, regardless of whether the overall temperature feels hot or cold to humans. Some areas, especially valleys with large creeks or rivers where moisture is likely to hang in the air at all times, can feel bone-chillingly cold, even when the thermostat rests well above freezing.

Pace Yourself

Humidity is not the only form of moisture we're likely to encounter when hitting the trails. The same mechanism meant to cool us off can backfire when the body is no longer active and the temperature is suddenly a whole lot colder. It is very important to control your rate of perspiration when hiking in the winter, because evaporative heat loss carries away more than just warmth—it essentially robs you of extra calories as well. Every gram of sweat that evaporates from your body steals both the energy it took to produce that sweat as well as the temperature loss from evaporation. Becoming overheated on a winter hike can often be just as dangerous as feeling cold. There is no more deadly a scenario than reaching the summit of a mountain drenched in sweat from your climb, only to find the temperature has dropped 20°F since the last time you checked. Mountain summits are frequently very windy places, and brutally cold 40 mph winds whipping up off the slopes can easily slip in through the gaps in your clothes, robbing you of your warmth. Such a scenario will turn your sweat-drenched body against itself, and it's therefore crucial to manage your perspiration levels throughout the course of a winter hike. If you find that you're beginning to sweat to the point that it's soaking into your clothes, it's time to take a short break and let yourself cool off. When you resume hiking, continue at a slower, less intensive pace so that you do not sweat as much. While the number one rule for a comfortable winter hike is to keep moving, it's important to amend this by adding that you should "keep moving" at a manageable pace that doesn't cause you to sweat, or at least, doesn't cause you to sweat much.

For those hikers who are intimidated by cold weather, this is all ultimately good news. Look at it this way: winter hiking may be challenging, but you're almost guaranteed to be warmer than you were before you started hiking, and in most scenarios, you're not allowed to push yourself too hard. Under warm weather conditions, many hardcore hikers tend to push on through the pain, rarely stopping for breaks even when they're gasping for breath and their legs feel like jelly. Others—probably most—are happy to pause and regain their strength as often as necessary. During the winter, everyone needs to be this second type of hiker. Force yourself to hike slowly and pause for regular rests so that your body temperature remains within a manageable comfort zone.

As a general rule, hikers should avoid cotton garments in the first place, but you should absolutely never wear cotton clothing on a winter hike. Cotton essentially collapses when wet, losing its insulating properties entirely. All clothing is doomed to lose some of its insulating capability when it becomes wet, and the wetter the clothing is, the less it can insulate. Cotton simply fails faster, and if the garment becomes soaked through, you'll basically be wearing a layer of water. Moisture, as we've established, is great at heat transfer. Picture the uncomfortable image of a person caught in a rainstorm, soaked through and thoroughly miserable. Their insulating clothing has been rendered useless, and there is essentially

no longer any opportunity for them to retain any body heat. Needless to say, this is not a situation you want to find yourself in while on top of a cold windy mountain in the snow.

The Layering Strategy

By now, it should hopefully be clear why simply wearing your warmest winter coat when setting out for a strenuous winter hike is a self-defeating strategy. While that coat may feel especially warm and cozy when you're simply walking around town, you'll quickly become *too* warm as you exert yourself. If you continue wearing this extra warm and cozy coat as you generate lots and lots of sweat, the inside of the coat will become soaked. By the time you reach the midpoint of your hike—the time when you'll likely need that warmth most—your own clothing may be working against you, leaching your body heat and casting it off into the mountain air. Instead, you'll need a more modular strategy.

Every body is different, and so there's no perfect layering strategy that will apply to anyone and everyone. Layering should be viewed not as a literal checklist for what to wear and when to wear it, but as a strategy, a skill that can be learned.

First, there's the base layer. This layer may seem simple, but it's easy to fall into the cotton trap here without realizing it. While your base layer under ordinary circumstances is likely as simple as just throwing on a t-shirt, such garments are often made of the materials that suffer the most from soaking up moisture. You've probably heard the term "moisture-wicking" in the context of athletic and outdoor gear, and this is exactly why such a concept is useful. When choosing cold-weather clothing, it's especially important to select a base layer made out of a moisture-wicking

Several lighter, more versatile layers are always preferable to a single heavy layer. While a thinner hiking jacket may not provide sufficient warmth entirely on its own, it's important to be able to add as well as remove layers in increments.

fabric like merino wool or a synthetic fiber (see more suggestions below). Merino wool tends to be more expensive than most synthetic fabrics, but has the advantage of being highly breathable, and supposedly doesn't hold as much odor as other types of fabric.

For most moderate hikes, I don't usually think about base layers beyond my shirt and gloves. And under more moderate weather conditions or for shorter, less extreme winter hikes, I'm usually plenty comfortable in just my regular hiking pants. For more extreme winter hikes, however, a base layer of moisture-wicking long underwear is worth considering.

Under ideal circumstances, most of your base layer of clothing is unlikely to change during your hike. (Unless you're attempting some kind of Polar Bear Challenge, but that's another story altogether, you maniac.) The exception to this may be your socks, which can become damp and uncomfortable quite easily, and have less opportunity to breathe than your other layers of clothing. While I do not commonly pause and change out my socks unless I'm camping or on a particularly long hike, I highly recommend carrying a few extra spare pairs, just in case. Hiking through snow with wet socks and wet feet is something you really, really want to avoid.

Above the base layer, all other layers should be considered for their modular qualities, as they may be swapped on and off several times throughout the hike. It is not uncommon at all for me to begin a hike with several or all of my layers, and to thereafter swap layers on and off multiple times, depending on my level of exertion.

After the base layer, the focus is on insulation. The insulating middle layer of garments will likely spend the most time getting swapped on and off your body as you hike. I prefer to wear a moisture-wicking long sleeve shirt above my base layer, as I often feel too warm to hike in a jacket, but too cold if I strip all the way down to my base layer short sleeve shirt. Granted, I do not get cold as easily as most, and many others may feel most comfortable wearing a light hiking jacket throughout the hike. Under extra cold conditions, for some hikers, both a long-sleeve shirt and jacket may be required, even with constant movement.

Regardless, despite the focus on insulation with this middle layer, you should still resist the urge to just throw on a nice warm winter jacket. However paradoxical it may sound, a lighter jacket will almost always serve you better. Consider that the lighter and more versatile each component of your layering system is, the more layers you can swap on and off. A good mid-layer jacket, when purchased from an outdoors outfitter specializing in this sort of thing, should be designed for the purpose of layering. These jackets will commonly either be made from fleece or a combination of water-resistant nylon exterior fabric with some sort of fill—look for jackets rated around 650-fill. Such jackets often have an adjustable hood, although this is not necessary if you've elected to wear a headband or beanie hat instead. You'll also want a jacket that's highly compressible and weighs very little, so that it's easier to take off and stuff in your pack. Chances are, your random winter jacket that you bought for commut-ing to work will not meet these requirements, which is why it's worth heading to a specialty outfitter to pick out your gear.

Finally, there's the outer layer. You'll often hear this layer referred to as the "shell," particularly in terms of jackets. Recall that each layer should be viewed as serving a specific purpose (though admittedly, they can blur together). The base layer is generally there to remove moisture and trap heat close to the skin. The middle layer is the insulation layer, regulating exactly how much heat we're keeping close or allowing to dissipate. The outer layer is the protective layer, and generally comes into play when faced with the harshest winter elements: strong winds, extreme temperatures, moisture in the form of rain, snow, or ice.

While this protective outer shell should ideally still be somewhat breathable—perhaps you'll be traversing an exposed mountain ridge with harsh winds, but while still exerting yourself strenuously—its main job is to prevent the elements from swooping in and stealing the insulating powers of your middle layer. The shell layer often does not need to provide a significant amount of additional insulation, as its main job is to protect the insulation you're already wearing. Other components of this layer may include sunglasses, heavy gloves, and bib pants with zippered sides. One might also consider face protection like a balaclava to be part of your shell, though a balaclava is also insulating. The designation does not matter, of course—the important thing is that you know the appropriate time to employ these garments.

When you feel the need to take a break to rest, don't wait to cool off before you add another layer. Add a layer immediately so that it'll trap your body heat. Your body will stop producing heat as you rest, and your temperature will drop off rapidly unless

Open, exposed summit areas are often prone to high winds and lower temperatures, which are mitigated by a good shell layer jacket.

you're properly insulated. Apply the same logic in reverse once you begin hiking again. Remove your outer-most layer before you start moving, otherwise you will quickly begin overheating, and you'll risk soaking your clothes in sweat. While starting out minus a layer may initially cause you to feel too cold, your body heat will very quickly make up the difference.

Such logic may not feel intuitive at first, so whether you're hiking with children or inexperienced adults, be mindful that everyone follows this practice. Momentary discomfort is well worth enduring in the name of safety. Every hiker finds their comfort level at a different pace, and thus, each

hiker will need to be vigilant when hiking in a group. Some members of the group will inevitably work up a sweat faster than others. Make sure that at least a few members of the group have ample experience and take charge to ensure that everyone is moving at a comfortable, safe pace.

Types of Clothing Material

It's easy to take the advances we've made in clothing technology for granted. The fabrics that our shirts and jackets are made from rarely inspire excitement like the latest smartphone or video game console. But consider that, not even 100 years ago, winter hiking truly would not have been the same casual activity that it is today. Equipped with only household garments, a layperson in the early 1900s was taking quite a risk any time they needed to wander miles from their home in the sub-freezing cold of winter. Much of the intimidation that we feel for hiking in the winter today, I believe, is the result of residual feelings from earlier eras, but it is possible to update our preferences. The advances we've made in materials and moisture control truly are game changing when it comes to winter activities.

WOOL

In the past, wool was the insulator of choice, replaced only with the advent of synthetic materials. Today, while wool remains a good option under many circumstances, its benefits have largely been surpassed and supplanted by other materials, though it is often still the cheapest option for a sturdy, reliable, warm garment. While wool retains the ability to trap heat even when wet, it also becomes quite heavy when wet, and dries slowly. Being that it is generally heavier and bulkier in the first place, it may take up significantly more pack room, and add noticeably to your overall weight load.

DOWN AND SYNTHETIC DOWN

Down is the light fluffy coating grown beneath the feathers of waterfowl, a natural insulator and protective layer. Unlike feathers, down has no quill. Because it is so warm, durable, compressible, and breathable, it is one of the most efficient lightweight insulating materials that we know of. But of course, there's always a catch. First, down must be taken from a waterfowl, so hikers should research the company they're purchasing from and ensure that the down is humanely sourced. Another drawback

Types of Clothing Material

Wool
Down
Synthetic Down
Fleece
Other Synthetics

of down is that it becomes nearly useless when wet. In much of the east coast or the Pacific Northwest, relying upon down as an insulator may pose more of a risk than a gain.

Synthetic down insulation is designed to replicate the qualities of down but retain its benefits even when wet. It's made with polyester fibers intertwined and arranged in differently sized filaments, mimicking down's lofty clusters. These ultrafine fibers trap heat in air pockets, providing great warmth—though still not quite insulating as effectively as real down. In addition, synthetic down insulation has a slightly higher weight-to-warmth ratio than real down, meaning it needs to be heavier to retain the same amount of heat. The upside to synthetic insulation is that it is much more resistant to moisture, and when it does get wet it dries faster. Unlike real down, synthetic insulation can dry within a day—sometimes even hours—if placed in the sun and/or wind.

FLEECE AND OTHER SYNTHETICS

Fleece is one of the oldest synthetic materials associated with outdoor recreation. Made from polyester, fleece is quite effective at trapping body heat, while also being comfortable and lightweight. Polyester fleece is also extremely durable and moisture resistant, which would seem to make it an ideal material for winter activities. The main downside of fleece, however, may simply be that it's difficult to determine the level of quality, as there are numerous types of fleece. Each type has significant differences in density, and therefore, significant variation in how well they insulate. The type of fleece best suited for winter recreation is usually called "polar fleece," and one should always be careful to check that the jacket you're relying on for your winter outing is indeed made from this particular material. If you are simply dragging an old jacket out of the basement and aren't able to find any particular information about the material, you may want to test this jacket out under milder conditions before relying on it for a serious winter expedition.

Due to its mass availability and affordability, fleece has become favored over wool by most casual hikers. Synthetic materials generally insulate similarly to wool, and dry more quickly. However, wet wool will generally keep one warmer than a wet synthetic, meaning both materials have advantages in certain applications.

Additionally, eco-conscious adventurers might notice that polyester is derived from petroleum products. To combat the effects of petroleum use, some companies now manufacture their polar fleece from recycled plastic. Synthetics may be derived from compounds other than polyester, as well, such as polypropylene, pile, polyethylene, and nylon. Different materials trap heat differently—polyester traps heat more effectively than polyethylene, which in turn is more effective than nylon.

Shell Layer Options

Your shell layer can be modified for multiple types of scenarios, depending on your environment and conditions. Sometimes your shell layer will need to maximize wind resistance, other times waterproofing, and sometimes breathability. Realistically, many times you'll want it to maximize all of the above if possible. A good technical shell jacket can be very expensive, however, and the average hiker cannot afford to purchase a different jacket for all situations. Often, simply understanding how to adapt your layering system will achieve the desired end result.

Because a single jacket can only do so much, you'll sometimes hear the strengths and weaknesses of different jackets broken down by "hard shell" and "soft shell" options. Soft shell jackets tend to offer superior ventilation, though they lack the waterproof capabilities of a hard-shell jacket. For less extreme environments where you may still encounter strong winds, limited exposure, and a temporary drop in temperature, you may not need much more than a windbreaker that will fit comfortably over your middle insulation layer. However, many materials used for insulating middle-layer jackets are increasingly effective at wind resistance on their own, meaning that hikers may want to focus on a shell layer that instead prioritizes comfort and water resistance. With a good middle insulation layer and a durable hard shell outer jacket, you should be able to endure changing conditions in all but the most extreme of environments.

In the most intense of winter hiking conditions, even a three-layer system may not be enough. In these situations, a fourth layer may be necessary.

A warm beanie hat or headband is a vital piece of winter gear, as your ears are one of the first places where you'll begin to feel the cold.

Generally, this layer should also prioritize insulation, and an additional mid-layer jacket can be called upon here.

Protecting Your Extremities

There's an old adage that you've probably heard at some point, claiming that most body heat is lost through our heads. While this claim happens to be false—heat loss from any part of the body generally occurs proportionally to how much skin is exposed—it can often *feel* true. The head, and, in my experience, the hands as well, are simply the most challenging parts of the body when it comes to regulating temperature. When exposed, they become cold very quickly, and yet a beanie hat or a jacket hood often insulates too well for the strenuous exercise performed during a hike. In my experience, the ideal insulator for the head during a moderate or even sub-freezing winter hike is often just a headband, at least while one is moving. A beanie or hood are usually only required once one enters the coldest, windiest portion of the hike. For, here is the other reason the head is claimed to lose heat so fast: its vulnerable sensory organs simply register discomfort far more easily. A freezing cold wind blasting away at your eyes and exposed ears will feel a lot more alarming than that same wind chipping away at your knees or elbows.

Nonetheless, while it's easy to focus on your jacket as the vital centerpiece of your shell layer, all parts of your body will likely require additional protection in those extreme conditions. For the majority of hikes, a lighter pair of winter gloves will often suffice. Such gloves maximize dexterity as you move about, adjust your gear, and add and remove layers. These gloves should still be water resistant, though often hikers will rely on an additional shell layer of glove or mitten for truly waterproofing their hands and insulating under colder conditions. Thus, heavy gloves or mittens often need to be worn over your thinner, liner gloves, and these heavier gloves may prioritize either warmth, water-resistance, or both. In the most extreme of conditions, you may need to layer gloves just as you'll layer jackets over your core, with thin liner gloves, a medium, insulating pair of gloves over these, and a final, shell layer of mitten for additional protection and resistance to snow and water.

A balaclava can provide additional warmth around the head and neck, while gaiters will serve the dual purpose of insulating your ankles and lower legs while keeping your feet dry and out of the snow. Sunglasses may be required simply to ward off the glare of the sun reflecting off the snow, but in the most intense of environments, snow goggles can be helpful in protecting your eyes.

While we've already mentioned carrying a backup pair of socks, in case your original pair becomes wet, if temperatures are low enough, you may wish to consider wearing two pairs of warm socks in the first place. Still, this strategy can only take you so far, and a sturdy pair of warm winter boots become important here. If you try to wear too many pairs of socks, your feet will be cramped and movement may become uncomfortable. If your feet are extremely cramped, it may even limit your blood circulation, which means your feet will actually get colder faster.

Boots

While a good pair of standard hiking boots may suffice for less intense winter hikes, or for trails where there is little or no snow, an expedition into the coldest, snowiest winter landscapes demands a more serious pair of shoes. Boots designed for winter hiking are insulated, should be sized to accommodate thicker (and/or layers of) socks, and will have a thicker sole to limit heat loss between your feet and the snow. Waterproof boots are generally preferred as well, since snow will inevitably melt, saturate your boot, and over a long enough hike, can eventually soak through your socks. Because hikers often set out for a winter hike wearing multiple pairs of socks due to varying temperatures and conditions, it can be a challenge to size your boots correctly for these circumstances. Winter hiking boots are certainly an item that's best purchased in-person, and it may be worthwhile to bring extra socks along to your fitting so that you can emulate conditions on the trail.

In addition to standard boots, there are many sub-varieties of winter boot for specific applications. Cross-country skis generally require specialized boots with additional support designed around a particular clasp system. Adventurers who push beyond mere hiking into actual mountain-

Sturdy, waterproof boots are a must for most winter outings, but should also be supplemented by gaiters and traction gear for full protection and grip on icy surfaces.

eering will discover that this breed of mountain-climber requires specialty boots as well, which tend to be far more sturdy, insulated, and expensive than your average winter boot. Such extreme footwear is beyond what most casual hikers will ever need, however.

Finally, on the "extremely casual" side of winter outings, mukluks may suffice in a pinch. Mukluks are the name for the casual boot most commonly associated with winter, generally worn for shovel-ing off the driveway, walking around the backyard or into town, or simply playing in the snow with children. These one-piece boots usually rise to a little below one's knee, or at least several inches above the ankle, and are designed for flexibility and comfort. However, mukluks are not meant for more extended outings, and their design often allows snow to work its way into the open space around one's leg, where it will eventually melt and soak into your socks.

Gaiters

Every hiker serious about hiking regularly in the winter should invest in a pair of gaiters. An accessory to your boots, gaiters simply slip over your boots, with a strap running under the arch of your foot. A protective shell covers your ankles and lower legs. Most gaiters offer some sort of drawstring or tightening mechanism to pinch tight at the top—their primary function, after all, is to cover up the openings at the top of your boots, so that snow cannot make its way down to your feet. A good pair of gaiters should be water resistant or waterproof, and adventurers heading out into more extreme environments may want gaiters that are insulated as well.

Glasses and Ski Goggles

Snow is reflective, and in direct sunlight, it can be blindingly bright. Sunglasses in winter might feel paradoxical to some. If you're hiking on a clear blue-sky day, however, and there's snow on the ground, chances are good that you'll need some form of eye protection. The same sunglasses you might wear for a summer hike should serve just fine in winter too. As always, the more extreme the environment, the more intense the gear you'll need. Those planning to hike up to higher altitude summits with significant exposure may need to pack a pair of ski goggles, not only to manage the sunlight off the snow, but to protect your eyes from the fierce mountain winds as well.

Opposite: Gaiters slip over your footwear and cover most of the lower leg, helping to keep snow out of your boots

Absaroka Beartooth Wilderness, Montana

Specialty winter gear opens up whole new adventure opportunities, such as exploring the backcountry of Yellowstone National Park, most of which is closed to vehicular traffic in the winter months.

4.

GEARING UP

Winter hiking is more complicated than summer hiking in nearly all respects, and that holds especially true when it comes to the gear involved. Some hikers—those who derive pleasure from researching and picking out the exact perfect gear for every situation—will savor this aspect of the season, while others may find the extra effort daunting, an additional barrier to hitting the trails. Regardless, this section is designed to provide you with as much information as possible, so that your selection process only requires as much time and effort as you care to put into it.

There is one caveat that generally holds true for almost all winter hiking considerations: the more extreme the conditions and terrain, the more effort you will have to put into preparing. For those just starting out, it's best to ease yourself into things with simple, well-trafficked trails that can be counted on to pose few unexpected dangers. Generally speaking, the easier and more straightforward your hike, the safer you'll be even when defaulting to the simplest, least technical gear options at a lower budget level. While you'll always want to be sure that you do have the proper gear for any scenario you might reasonably expect to encounter on your hike, the simplest of hikes at least tend to narrow this spectrum greatly. Once you are ready to tackle rougher and more remote trails in winter, you'll be able to take the knowledge and confidence you've gained and apply it when picking out more advanced or technical winter hiking gear.

Of course, there is a secondary question separate from the hike's degree of difficulty: what part of the country are you planning to hike in, and how much snow does that area generally receive? Such considerations have already been covered in other chapters, but this knowledge must be had in order to determine exactly what sort of gear you'll need to pack for your hike. Some parts of the country rarely get any snow, making snowshoes, for instance, largely irrelevant. While this example may seem like obvious common sense, planning for your winter adventure isn't always so easy to intuit. If you live in a part of the country that rarely receives snow, where snowshoes appear irrelevant, you might assume that this same logic applies to other winter hiking gear as well. Yet winter weather and terrain can be very tricky, and icy patches of trail have a habit of popping up when you least expect them, stubbornly persisting well into the spring. Because of this, I believe almost all winter hikers—with the exception perhaps of those dwelling in the warmest non-mountainous regions, like Florida—should own a pair of microspikes.

Microspikes and Other Traction Devices

Above all other equipment, a pair of spikes is often the single most impactful piece of gear for tackling the widest range of conditions. From the deserts of the southwest to the muddy woods of the Mid-Atlantic, you are likely to encounter an icy trail at some point almost anywhere you go. The winter when I bought my first pair of spikes was a winter that completely changed how I see the seasons, shifting winter all at once from a time of drudgery to a period of adventure. The ability to confidently walk over a sheet of pure ice almost feels like a superpower. The first time you do so, it's so uncanny as to be a nearly magical experience. Even after years of winter hiking, it never really ceases to amaze.

The terminology around traction gear can be a bit of a mess, and you'll often hear hikers refer to all flavors of traction footwear as "crampons." I've been guilty of doing this myself, and while it perhaps makes little difference in a casual conversation, there are important technical differences between the different types of traction gear that you should understand while doing your shopping. You might easily put yourself in danger if you're attempting a hike that necessitates crampons, and all you brought were a cheap pair of coil-based Yaktrax.

Yaktrax is one manufacturer of a very common type of traction device, which crisscross metal springs around the bottom of your boot. This design is usually the most affordable option, and as a result, has become quite popular, to the point that many people simply refer to all versions of this type of device as Yaktrax, the way many people refer to all brands of lip balm as Chapstick. Yaktrax slip over your boots, just like most traction devices, but tend to be cheaper and are thus engineered for less intensive conditions. The "coils" do not grip ice as well as spikes do, and therefore these should only be used in areas where ice is patchy, soft, or broken up. On solid slick ice, you will still run a high risk of falling or sliding.

Microspikes also slip over your boot but utilize—you guessed it—spikes. Unlike crampons, the spikes on microspikes are not fixed in place, but built into chains that hug the bottom of your boot. Really, microspikes function much like tire chains, just for a boot rather than a large automobile tire. This makes them light, compact, and easy to transport, but also means they're somewhat easier to break. The chains of your spikes will sometimes get caught on a stray branch or rock, and you'll have to be mindful not to get tripped up as you walk. The spikes will also wear out over time if you're constantly smashing them against rocks, so I usually try to only wear my spikes for the portions of a

It is always a good idea to carry spikes or crampons in your bag, especially when hiking on a trail that covers a wide variety of terrain.

hike where I know they'll be needed. Fortunately, microspikes are compact and easily fit into a bag, so again, I advise all winter hikers to carry them along just in case.

Like microspikes, most **crampons** are designed to harness onto your boots, but crampons tend to be more rigid in their design. Whereas microspikes merely wrap around your boot, crampons have spikes fixed into a solid platform that straps onto your boot. Crampons can attach to your boot with a tension lever or bind to your boot with a strap system. In practical terms, crampons usually feature larger spikes, and the fact that these spikes are set into a rigid platform usually means better grip and more support. Good crampons can

capably tackle a steeply angled icy surface where other traction devices might still slide. However, crampons are less compact than microspikes, and are often more difficult to equip, especially while out in the field. Most entry level crampons can be adapted to the average sturdy winter hiking boot, though crampons also scale for the greatest extremes of winter adventuring. Serious mountaineers and ice climbers need traction too, and these top-of-the-line devices are often designed to match with specialized boots. The average hiker will not require such technical gear, however, and in the majority of circumstances, the flexibility and portability of microspikes makes them a better option.

The Necessity of Deep-Snow Gear

First, a note on snowshoeing and cross-country skiing. When does traveling up a mountain on foot for fun cease to be hiking, and become something else? Are snowshoeing and cross-country skiing variations on hiking, fine-tuning the activity using specialized tools for particular environments, or is it important to classify them as something else altogether?

Personally, I don't think this semantic distinction is particularly important or meaningful under most circumstances. I only raise it here because I believe it often serves as a soft psychological barrier to exploring winter activities for many hikers. Skiing often seems to be viewed as the quintessential winter activity, and as a result, it can feel as if those who have a hesitation to go skiing may end up feeling a hesitation to go outside in the winter at all. I've never been a skier or a snowboarder, and I can definitely recall a time when it just didn't feel like going outside in the winter was an option, because what would I even do? But the truth is that skiing and snowshoeing can be viewed as their own distinct pursuits, or they can be seen as mere tools, methods of enabling a more open-ended approach to winter recreation. For the more casual hiker who tends to shy away from skiing and snowboarding, the use of snowshoes and cross-country skis should be viewed as simply a compliment to winter hiking, tools to be called upon under the right conditions.

In most parts of the country, snowshoes and skis aren't always necessary. There's likely a park near you in a low-lying area that doesn't receive a ton of snow, where you'll simply be able to hike and saunter on foot. However, there are some areas where exploring in winter without the use of snowshoes or cross-countries skis may not be an option. Some parks groom their trails exclusively for cross-country ski use in the winter. Many mountainous areas forbid hiking without snowshoes in the winter based on the depth of the snow—any more than about 8 inches usually necessitates the use of snowshoes or skis.

On mountains that are high in elevation or located in northern regions, snow becomes so deep that a hiker without snowshoes may find themselves physically unable to move down the trail. If the snow is deep enough, this can create a dangerous situation, particularly if such deep snow is concentrated mostly around summits but not at lower elevations. On a hike in New York's Adirondack Mountains, for example, one might find the majority of the trail to be completely free of snow and ice as soon as early spring. And yet after hiking for miles in balmy, sunny spring conditions, you may still suddenly encounter vast drifts of snow in shaded areas around the summit, which remain so deep that you'll sink up to your waist unless you came equipped with snowshoes. This can be especially problematic if you were cutting it close with your time estimations; an 8-hour day of hiking can easily become drawn out into a 12-hour day.

Postholing

No matter how much experience you have as a hiker, you will never be able to make much progress hiking through snow that comes up to your waist, much less up to your neck. Even in less extreme conditions, trudging through knee-height snow poses other issues, not only for you but for other

Hiking through deep snow without snowshoes or skis will leave a torn-up trail riddled with "postholes," deep pockets of collapsed snow that make movement even more challenging for hikers attempting to traverse the trail afterward.

hikers as well. As each footstep punches through the snow, it leaves behind a hole, which will eventually freeze over and harden during subsequent freeze-thaw cycles. Your path through the snow thus eventually becomes something like a road littered with ragged potholes. This phenomenon is called "postholing," and it can ruin a trail for the hikers who come after you. Not only does it butcher the smooth yet fragile blanket of snow, but it is a miserable, exhausting experience for the hiker doing the postholing as well. With each footstep, you will suddenly find the ground giving way beneath you like quicksand. Sometimes, you may end up crossing a stretch of firmer, compacted snow and feel as if you've finally found solid ground, but this is often a mirage.

Snow is finicky and complex, as we will explore in chapter 6, and you will rarely be able to guess when you are standing on solid ground versus a snowpack that's ready to collapse under your weight. Inevitably, you will find yourself pitching forward as your leg vanishes into the snow beneath you. You may find yourself lurching to the side, thrown off balance, or toppling forward face-first into the snow. You will pull your leg out and push forward, only to do it all over again—step after step after step, with no relief in sight. To make matters worse, the force of your leg pushing in and out and in and out of deep snow will inevitably force snow down your boots, no matter how effectively you've protected your legs with gaiters. Thus, you will not only find yourself exerting ten times the effort to move forward, but you will be doing so with increasingly cold, wet, uncomfortable feet.

Postholing is no good for anyone. Snowshoes and skis are the best solution.

Snowshoes

Snowshoes and skis are the only effective way to traverse deep snow on foot in winter. Both rely on the same basic principle of dispersing your weight over a much greater surface area than your feet otherwise ever could. Both are very ancient technologies that mankind has relied on in northern climates for many thousands of years—at least eight millennia. The indigenous people of North America were particularly adept at developing snowshoe technology, with a variety of designs for varying conditions and types of terrain.

Picture the classic design of a snowshoe, with a bent-wood frame and a webbing of strips. This archetypal snowshoe developed by indigenous peoples was readily adopted by European trappers, settlers, and soldiers, and soon spread across the world. Around the 1950s, when innovations in outdoor recreation technology began to speed up, designs emerged for a more sturdy, modern snowshoe, with technological adaptations like a pivoting binding and crampons for traction. Today, snowshoes are often far more specialized, with options for running, mountaineering, and casual hiking alike.

RECREATIONAL SNOWSHOES serve as the entry-level option for all-purpose winter hiking. The most basic of recreational snowshoes are designed primarily for flat terrain and low rolling hills. These budget snowshoes are meant for less intensive use, which allows for a simpler overall design. Such snowshoes generally utilize a more rudimentary binding system and offer less aggressive traction. Nonetheless, there are variations within even the most basic type of snowshoes that are worth noting. Some feature rounded ends,

Snowshoes are necessary for winter hikes in many areas of the country where deep and variable snow cover can be expected, such as the Rocky Mountains.

Snowshoes engineered for use in the backcountry typically feature a sturdy, easily adjustable binding system as well as a heel lift, allowing for easier movement up steep slopes.

which are better for distributing weight, while others are tapered to enable a more natural walking gait. Binding systems can vary from model to model and brand to brand, and different binding systems may appeal to different hikers based on convenience, comfort, as well as personal preference.

BACKCOUNTRY SNOWSHOES are engineered for more challenging expeditions into backcountry areas or extended backpacking treks where hikers will be carrying heavier weight loads. More expensive and more technical, such snowshoes are ideal for hikers who frequently head to the mountains but will likely be unnecessary for those who tend to stick to rolling hills and open fields. Those who plan to hike regularly in mountainous terrain should probably save up for a decent, well-engineered pair, as snowshoes can be cumbersome to use, and a cheap, poorly designed pair of snowshoes will quite literally trip you up. Pay particular attention to the various binding systems used by different companies, and what reviewers say about their ease of use. Many hikes will require snowshoes only for some

portion of the trail, meaning you may have to take them on and off again at least once, and perhaps several times. Ease of use is thus crucial. You'll also need to make sure that your backpack has some sort of strap system for carrying your snowshoes when you aren't wearing them.

RUNNING SNOWSHOES are becoming increasingly popular as technology improves and as more people place emphasis on fitness as much as exploration. Perhaps unthinkable even a century ago, technology has changed so much in recent decades that snowshoes have shrunk dramatically in both size and weight, to the point of some newer models being almost unrecognizable as snowshoes. Trail running in general is growing more popular every year, and for many, a thick cover of snow in the winter is no excuse to take the season off. Nonetheless, it isn't yet possible for a single design to conquer every type of terrain, and running snowshoes are not meant for serious expeditions or rugged terrain. These snowshoes prioritize speed and movement over flotation and traction. They tend to be shorter and narrower than standard snowshoes, and allow the runner to adopt a more natural gait. Nonetheless, in a less mountainous region where the trails are flatter and generally easier to traverse, these snowshoes can still serve just fine as your everyday pair.

Basics of Cross-Country Skiing

Cross-country skiing is difficult to learn. The first time you try it, you will very likely feel totally humiliated, curse the futility of the pursuit, and feel tempted to quit after about 20 minutes. At least, that's how it went for me. I had the

Grafton Notch State Park, Maine

misfortune of heading to a park that was quite a bit more hilly than I had anticipated, and this is not where you want to learn to cross-country ski. Find somewhere flat. Also, find somewhere where you will not be surrounded by hordes of young children who are already expert skiers. These dozens of tireless, annoyingly nimble youth will ski circles around you as if it were the easiest, most natural thing in the world, which it certainly is not. Learning how to cross-country ski is quite challenging, primarily because you will spend at least an hour tripping over your own feet as if it were the first day in your life you ever tried to use your legs.

If you for some reason find the experience easier than I did, I would rather you not tell me about it, because I already feel embarrassed enough as it is.

If you wish to learn how to ski, do so in an environment where the trail conditions are easy and predictable, where you won't feel ashamed by your failures, and where you'll have plenty of time to break yourself in. Learning to ski with a partner can be very helpful, so long as that partner is patient and willing to take their time with you as you get your sea legs (or ski legs, as it were). The rewards are worth it. Skis open up even more of the backcountry in winter than snowshoes, as one can travel much faster, particularly on the return downhill. Most experienced skiers feel that cross-country skiing requires less effort than snowshoeing, since there is less resistance—you are gliding across the snow, rather than stomping through it. Nonetheless, there are certainly pros and cons of each. Skiing is much more difficult to learn than snowshoeing, and skis are far more cumbersome all around than snowshoes. While it's not entirely unreasonable to strap snowshoes on the back of your pack "just in case," transport-

ing cross-country skis is a whole other matter entirely. So while skis undoubtedly excel under certain particular conditions, they simply aren't as versatile all around.

Just as with snowshoes, there are different types of skis for different situations and technical levels. In addition to cross-country (or Nordic) skis, the trails you intend to ski may require backcountry skis, telemark skis, or alpine touring skis. These are all different in turn from downhill skis, the key difference being that touring skis keep a skier's heel free, particularly while ascending, to allow for a natural hiking or stepping motion.

Types of Skis

Different varieties of skis are available for all manner of conditions. Your local outdoor outfitter is the best place to learn about these different types of skis, and determine which are best for your purpose. Most styles of skiing, including basic cross-country skiing, should not be attempted without training and prior practice.

Basic cross-country or Nordic skis are long, thin, and light, designed to be very fast and smooth when traversing flat terrain. However, due to their lightweight and streamlined designs, these skis are only really suited to groomed trails or the tamest of backcountry trails. Skinny cross-country skis will not fare well on rugged terrain, so if no one has broken trail before you, you will likely find yourself exerting a great deal more effort than you anticipated, and unable to cover as much ground as you'd planned. Likewise, the bindings on such skis are generally not designed for steep downhill descents, so don't take skis like these out to a large, rugged peak expecting a swift, quick glide back down.

Because cross-country skis are limited in use,

The mountainous west offers many opportunities for alpine skiing, though such an activity should only be undertaken by those with sufficient training and experience.

they are ideal if you only plan to hike in an area where you know that the trails are consistently groomed, and where there is no real chance that you will be venturing off onto more rugged terrain. For cross-country skis, consistency is key. In the backcountry, however, conditions can vary widely, and change quickly. Depending on sunlight and shade, elevation, and underlying terrain, fluffy fresh powder may suddenly transition to wet slush or icy, hard snow out of nowhere.

Such unpredictable conditions demand skis that are able to handle a wide range of terrain. In this environment, you'll be better off with backcountry skis, sometimes referred to as touring skis. (Though not to be confused with alpine touring skis, which are meant for an even more extreme environment). Backcountry skis are shorter, wider, and float better over deep snow, making them far better suited to traversing unpredictable wilderness terrain. These skis also tend to be heavier and more expensive than cross-country skis, so you'll want to be sure that you truly require them (and enjoy using them) before acquiring a pair.

Poles for Hiking and Skiing

Any novice hiker first hitting the trail who spots a group of older adventurers ambling along with hiking poles almost always has the thought: "Well, I don't need that!" And it's true, to an extent—if you are young and in good shape, you probably don't need hiking poles. But wow, do they help, at least for the steepest, rockiest, craggiest trails. Hike long enough, and you can't help but notice how much of a difference poles can make. They take far more of the weight burden off of your legs, and knees in particular, than seems possible. They help with balance

on rocky trails, and on slick terrain. If you've already become a convert to hiking poles, then I probably don't have to explain why they're so important when hiking in winter.

Still, you won't need poles for every single hike. Generally, if I am hiking a trail that I know won't be icy or rocky, I don't always bring them along. If I'm hiking a trail that *is* steep and rocky, or that may be icy, I almost always bring poles. As a general rule, if you don't know a lot about the trail in question, use your intuition to estimate whether the trail might be snowy or icy or wet (or some combination of all of these). In such instances, bring your poles. When it comes to ensuring good traction and balance, poles are the second most important piece of gear after spikes. In addition, their typical benefits become even more relevant when hiking through snow: hikers usually carry more weight in the winter, and exert more effort when hiking over snowy ground.

You'll never regret owning a pair of good hiking poles, and you'll (probably) never regret bringing them along for a winter hike. As with most things gear related, however, there are multiple types of poles to choose from. For our purposes at the moment, there are essentially two types of poles to consider: compactable hiking poles and fixed-length ski poles.

Most hiking poles have some mechanism for collapsing or folding, so that they can be more easily packed away when not in use. In most cases, this same mechanism also allows the poles to be adjustable, so that hikers of all heights may comfortably use them. However, such adjustable poles usually employ a telescoping mechanism (so named for the way each section of the pole is designed to slide inside of the next), which can only handle so much

Hiking poles are tremendously helpful when hiking through a winter landscape, especially if icy terrain is involved.

weight. Some poles are made to fold like the supports of a tent, but these too suffer from weak joints that can't handle excessive pressure. This is even more of an issue when skiing, when the pressure being placed upon the poles is greater than it would be from simply walking.

Adventurers who plan to go cross-country skiing will need to invest in a pair of fixed-length poles for the activity. Cross-country ski poles are typically much longer than standard hiking poles, and are designed to handle the large amounts of pressure that cross-country skiing places on the shaft of the pole. In this case, telescoping or folding poles simply will not hold up to the task.

The Weight of Winter Hiking

Winter hiking often involves a lot of stuff, as you've perhaps already noticed. I myself own several backpacks: a casual bag for holding camera gear on less intensive outings, a daypack designed for comfort and versatility that I bring on the vast majority of my hikes, and a backpacking pack, for overnight and multi-day hikes. In winter, the challenge is often whether I can cram everything I need for a hike into my daypack, or whether to toss it all into my larger camping backpack while accepting that I'll be left with plenty of awkwardly unused room.

Adding to the challenge is the fact that most

winter gear is quite cumbersome, and often difficult to pack in a way that's even remotely convenient—think ice axes, skis, and snowshoes. Hand warmers and a few extra layers of clothing might pack nicely into your bag alongside your lunch and camera, but you'll need to be extra careful when packing something like an ice ax or snowshoes to ensure that their sharp points will only strike the ground in case you trip.

The solution, unfortunately, is usually to just play it safe, and go bigger than you may really need. When it comes to winter hiking (though really, this is true of any wilderness adventure), it's usually better to be over rather than under prepared. If heading out for a hike in a remote area where you might become lost—especially if you're hiking alone or hiking in a group where no one has much familiarity with the trails you'll be taking—it's often a good idea to pack a sleeping bag and other emergency supplies, as well as additional layers and extra pairs of socks. For the same reason, you'll want to pack extra food, and in more extreme cases, fire starting tools as well. All of this in addition to your snowshoes and other winter gear means that you'll be faced with a tradeoff between a lighter, easier hike with some real risks should things go wrong, and a hike where you'll be carrying far more weight but will be prepared in case of an emergency. Packing even a couple of the above items will add quite a bit of weight to your pack, and it's simply not reasonable to try to carry so much gear on a relatively tame trail.

What sort of hikes are potentially dangerous enough to warrant the load? Admittedly, there's no simple answer to this question, and you'll have to develop your own intuition for when such measures are worth the effort. You'll notice that that's a running theme throughout this book, but when it comes to many wilderness skills, intuition is really

the ultimate form of knowledge at the end of the day. Many situations in the wild can unfold in unpredictable and erratic ways, and adapting to such circumstances will never be a purely straightforward skill.

For me, the basic questions to ask are: how familiar am I with this particular trail? Do I feel confident that I know roughly what obstacles to expect, and is it possible there will be stretches of trail that are unexpectedly more dangerous than anticipated? If I slip and sprain my ankle, how difficult will it be to limp back out the way I came? How likely am I to still have cell reception throughout the hike?

Developing the skill and intuition to answer these questions and pack appropriately simply requires experience. The only way to safely build experience is to set out for hikes where you do feel comfortable, and after testing yourself, begin to push your boundaries further.

Backpacks

There are an enormous variety of hiking backpacks available on the market today, but fortunately, it's not too difficult to intuit what sort of backpack will be appropriate for the adventure at hand. While finding a backpack that fits perfectly and remains comfortable when loaded with heavy gear can be a challenge, the best way to tackle this challenge is to simply head to an outdoor outfitter that you trust, where you can try on a selection of backpacks with the help of an experienced guide.

The main question to ask yourself when looking for a backpack is: can it hold all your stuff (without being considerably bigger than you actually need)? This, of course, requires you to first have a rough idea of what you'll need to carry, which can vary drastically depending on the type of expedition you're planning. And it's not the only consideration,

Your backpack should be selected not merely based on its carrying capacity, but also based on how easily you'll be able to access the gear and clothing you need. For easier and more moderate hikes, you'll generally want a versatile daypack that allows for easy, quick retrieval of commonly used gear and clothing items.

of course. Regardless of the size of pack you decide to go with, there are several factors that will determine how comfortable any given pack will be, and how easy it will be to load it up with accessories and cumbersome gear.

Almost all backpacks designed for anything but the most casual of hikes now come with a hip belt. A hip belt helps to distribute the load on your back elsewhere, so that your shoulders and upper back don't have to do all the work. Hips happen to be perfectly situated on the human body to absorb a good bit of that load, but a hip belt needs to be fitted and properly adjusted in order to accomplish this. The difference is immediately noticeable. Most

packs with a hip belt will also have a sternum strap. This strap, while generally much flimsier than a hip belt, nonetheless does a great bit of work in stabilizing the load and keeping the pack tight on your body. The snugger the fit, the better distributed the weight will be—plus, you'll be able to move a lot more fluidly when your backpack isn't swaying and bouncing around with every movement, constantly throwing off your balance.

Nearly all backpacks sold today utilize an internal frame system, which helps to redistribute the weight of the pack across your back and off your shoulders. However, some cheaper or more casual daypacks will not have an internal frame, and will

While only necessary under very specific conditions, an ice axe can make navigating certain icy areas far safer and easier.

thus become more uncomfortable than you might expect when loaded with extra gear, especially if you plan on strapping snowshoes or an ice axe onto them. Even higher end daypacks often do utilize an internal frame these days, however, and as a result of this extra support, I'm usually able to stuff my daypack completely full and still strap snowshoes onto the back without issue.

Different backpacks utilize different systems for strapping and adjusting gear externally. Higher end daypacks and backpacking packs typically have a versatile system of adjustable straps and loops so that you'll be able to securely tie down snowshoes or skis, though this may require a few additional straps to make sure they're truly snug. How complex of a strap system you'll need will likely depend on the range of activities you're planning to attempt. Adventurers who intend to do a lot of backcountry skiing, for instance, will require a bag with much greater capacity and versatility versus a hiker who intends only to get out for casual hikes but who may, once or twice a year, rely on snowshoes to navigate deeper snow. Fortunately, most hiking backpacks are versatile enough that you'll be able to start out with whatever you already own and expand your options from there.

Ice Axes

Ice axes may seem like an extreme measure, a tool to be used only during the most daunting of mountaineering adventures. While it's true that you'll likely never need an ice axe if you hike across primarily low-lying terrain, you'll be surprised by how often an ice axe becomes a crucial tool for navigating an iced-over trail in the mountains. What matters is not the height of the mountain, but the ruggedness and steepness of its trails. While the Catskill Mountains or Appalachians may seem diminutive compared to the giant summits of the Rocky Mountains and elsewhere, the low, eroded mountains of the East Coast nonetheless sport extremely craggy, rocky trails that frequently transform into icy flumes over the course of the winter. Further to the north, the White Mountains of New Hampshire are not all that much higher in elevation but receive even more regular snow and see persistently low temperatures, meaning ice is all but certain along much of the trail. Anywhere where you might find yourself climbing a steep grade of trail under icy conditions, it's possible that the trail could be entirely untraversable without the use of an ice axe.

Ice axes will almost always be used at the same time as spikes or crampons, since your feet are, obviously, your main point of contact with an icy surface. In addition to helping you climb steep, icy trails, ice axes are also the best way to halt an uncontrolled fall (a technique referred to as a glissade) in winter conditions. Of course, ice axes are sharp and, as mentioned previously, must be carefully secured to your pack so that you don't risk falling onto them and injuring yourself or others. Before entering a situation where glissading is a real possibility, seek out in-person training and guidance to better understand proper glissade techniques and precautions.

Chemical Hand and Toe Warmers

Chemical hand and toe warmers can be a lifesaver in the winter. Perhaps not literally, though there certainly are situations where it feels like you really might lose a finger or two without some kind of intervention. Since chemical warmers are lightweight and easy to carry, it's always worth tossing several in your bag when you head out for a winter hike. And be sure to pack several: on multiple occasions, I really needed a boost of heat, only to find that a packet of warmers simply wasn't warming. Usually, you'll be able to find other ways to warm your hands up sufficiently, and simply marching onward is generally enough to produce all the body heat that you'll need. Nonetheless, you don't want to get caught cold footed and unprepared.

For those who plan to hike (or ski, or any other activity) regularly in the winter, it's also worth considering investing in a set of electric handwarmers. While bulkier and heavier than chemical hand warmers, these battery-powered devices are convenient all around, as most also function as a battery backup, and in some cases, as a flashlight. While more expensive initially than their chemical counterparts, they are more than worth keeping in your gear kit for the long run.

But, back to chemical hand warmers. How does smacking a packet of plastic generate so much heat? It's worth remembering that heat, in the context of physics, is essentially a waste byproduct, the result of entropy. Even the most efficient of lightbulbs generate a small amount of waste heat, while old-school incandescent bulbs cast off nearly as much waste warmth as they do light. Chemical handwarmers operate thanks to a similar principle, except the heat generated by these packets is the result of, believe it or not, rust. Almost every brand of warmers contain the same basic ingredients: cellulose, iron, activated carbon, vermiculite, and salt, all sealed in a porous pouch. Upon activation, the heating process is generated by the exothermic oxidation of iron from exposure to air—and that process is simply the process of rusting. Strange as that may sound, these packets can produce sustained temperatures over 100°F and they'll do so for as long as the oxidization lingers, usually up to several hours. Be careful when placing a handwarmer inside your gloves or under your clothing—if the packet runs hot, over a sustained period of time, it can cause burns.

Ten Essentials

You may not always need everything in the following list on every hike, but this list isn't meant to suggest that you pack each of these every time. Rather, before every winter hike, read through this list and ensure that, first, you do have everything you need, and secondly, you know what you don't need, and why you don't expect to need it. While you shouldn't carry wholly unnecessary weight, you do need to be prepared for a number of unpredictable scenarios out on the trail.

1. **WARMTH:** Above all else, check to make sure you haven't forgotten to pack any crucial items of clothing. You'll need a layering system that can handle unpredictable weather conditions, a good hat or headband, and extra pairs of socks. Packing a few handwarmers is always a good idea too.

2. **NAVIGATION:** In winter, ensuring that you can find the trail (and stick to it without getting disoriented) is key. Make sure your cell phone is charged, download the trail map ahead of time, but don't count on your electronics. Bring a map and compass as a backup—and make sure you know how to use them first!

3. **FOOD AND WATER:** Pack enough food to sustain you through a full day in the outdoors, and more, if your route is more adventurous. For hydration, as a general rule, you'll need about half a liter of water for every hour of hiking. For most moderate excursions, about two liters of water should suffice. Bring your water in a well-insulated container so that it won't freeze. If you plan to hike for longer than five hours, or you're heading into a remote backcountry area, pack a filter, sterilizing tablets, or another method of purifying water.

4. **TRACTION GEAR:** You'll almost always want to pack a pair of microspikes, even if there's no snow on the ground in your neighborhood. Hiking poles are usually a good idea too.

5. **SUN PROTECTION:** If the sun is out and there's snow on the ground, you'll need sunglasses and sunscreen just as much as you would in summer.

6. **ILLUMINATION:** There's always a chance you'll get caught out after dark. Pack a headlamp and double check that the batteries in all your devices are fully charged.

7. **FIRST AID KIT:** No matter what time of year it is, packing a first aid kit is a good idea. Make sure nothing is missing or expired, and familiarize yourself with everything inside before you actually need to use it.

8. **KNIFE OR MULTI-TOOL:** Helpful in numerous situations!

9. **FIRE KIT:** Pack a lighter, matches, and perhaps even some fire starters.

Ten Essentials

1. Warmth
2. Navigation
3. Food and Water
4. Traction Gear
5. Sun Protection
6. Illumination
7. First Aid Kit
8. Knife or Multi-Tool
9. Fire Kit
10. Knowledge
★ **BONUS** Shelter

10. **KNOWLEDGE:** Where will you be hiking? How confident are you regarding trail conditions there? How long will it take you to return to your car if you realize, for whatever reason, that you won't be able to complete your hike?

★ **BONUS SHELTER:** It's simply not realistic to carry every possible piece of gear you might ever need on every single hike. Some trails, frankly, simply don't warrant the effort. If I'm going out for a casual hike in an area that I know well, I usually don't lug a sleeping bag and tent along with me as a backup safety measure. This all comes down to knowledge and intuition, however. You'll have to trust your own awareness and instincts to know when this cumbersome but helpful backup plan is worth the extra effort (and considerable weight).

Late winter transitions into spring in the Adirondack Mountains of New York.

5.

CAMPING IN THE COLD

Why in the world would you go camping in winter? This, I'm sure, is a question many would wonder when first seeing the title of this section. And it's not an unreasonable question—it's one that I have to admit I struggle with myself from time to time. Why slog through a whole backpacking trip in sub-freezing temperatures when I could instead set out for a long day hike and afterward head back home for a hot shower and the comfort of my warm bed? It takes a lot to motivate myself to spend a night in a tent on a frigid mountain, especially when darkness creeps in many hours before I'm able to fall asleep. Why take so many extra risks?

I say all this to assure you that I completely understand your skepticism. Why go camping in winter? Honestly, most people never will. The truth is, this is an activity that is not to be taken lightly, and requires a great deal of experience with winter hiking, winter weather, and gear. If you have the knowledge and preparation required to go on a winter camping expedition, chances are, you don't need me to give you permission.

For those (many) of you still on the fence, let me just say that there can be a perverse pleasure in conquering something so innately challenging as camping in the cold. That same thrill of adventure is what calls many of us to head out into the wilderness to go backpacking, despite its discomforts, in the first place. The same urge to dismantle limitations spurs many climbers on to tackle imposing rock faces. Humans do some pretty wild things, and camping in the winter probably wouldn't even rank in the top ten of the most extreme. Plus, once you muster the fortitude to experience it, there is an undeniable delight in watching the sun stain the snow red across the mountains, sinking into the purple twilight, and knowing that you have nowhere else to be. Then you're watching the stars come out above the peaks, and relishing the snow gleaming under the light of only the stars and the moon. The beauty of winter is never more ethereal nor more strangely fragile. Nothing highlights the transitive nature of winter better than a sunrise across the frozen landscape, and nothing challenges your own will to explore like a frigid night in a snowed-in tent.

Your Tent Makes All the Difference

Do you already own a tent for camping? If so, the first question you must ask is whether your tent is designed for backpacking or simply for car camping. If you aren't sure, or if you bought whatever tent you could find for cheap from a big retailer, chances are it's a basic tent meant only for camping in a campground.

If you bought your tent specifically for backpacking, on the other hand, you likely already know its limitations. This same loose principle also applies to sleeping bags. You probably know if you bought a sleeping bag designed for backpacking, because it likely cost a good bit more money and required research into temperature ratings and other technical specifics. In both cases, tents and sleeping bags engineered for wilderness camping will weigh much less than their casual equivalents. They'll also pack down into a small stuff sack and fit easily into a backpack. If your tent or sleeping bag is heavy and bulky, it is likely not designed for wilderness camping and should never be used for such. For one thing, it's probably too bulky for you to carry around for miles in the first place. But more importantly, such sleeping bags are not designed with the same insulation rating and material quality as backpacking bags and may become dangerously compromised if conditions are too cold or wet.

Once you've determined this, there's still another big question to ask, and this one may be even more crucial. If you now know that you have a three-season backpacking tent, do you wish to take the steps to winterize your tent, or do you want to buy yet another tent designed specifically for winter camping? Because here's the bad news: even a good (and likely expensive) three-season tent won't hold up to the roughest of winter weather on its own. Here's the even worse news: tents designed for winter camping cost a lot of money and aren't even particularly good as multi-purpose tents. Tents meant to be used during the warm-weather months are designed with abundant ventilation, while winter tents are engineered for heat retention, as you might expect. This, however, makes them quite stuffy and unpleasant when used during the summer, so you almost certainly won't want to use your winter tent for summer camping, and it may not be especially great for spring or fall either, depending on the climate where you live.

All this is to say, you probably only want to consider buying a winter tent if you are seriously dedicated to doing lots of camping in the winter. And if you're only now learning the basic of winter camping, chances are you can't realistically know yet how enthusiastically you'll wish to pursue it. Unless you have the spare change to toss nearly a thousand dollars at a fancy new tent you may rarely ever use, you'll probably want to find a way to test out winter camping first.

While warmth is paramount, winter tents are designed for more than just heat retention. After all, if heat retention were the only challenge to overcome, winter camping could, theoretically, be as simple as just packing extra layers to bundle up in overnight. Similar to the shell layer of your clothing, your winter tent needs to not only pro-

Most backpacking tents, such as the three-season tent pictured here, are not designed with winter camping in mind, but can can still be used by taking a few extra precautions.

vide insulation, but also needs to ensure that fierce winter winds won't pry away your hard-earned warmth through every gap and crack. Which, in turn, means that a winter tent needs to hold up to strong winds, and many of the basic design elements of a three-season tent simply won't cut it without some modifications.

ALTERNATIVES TO WINTER TENTS

Here's the good news: it is possible to make these modifications to a standard three-season tent. It may cost a little money, but it definitely won't cost as much as outright buying an expensive winter tent. For the casual camper, and especially those who live in regions where winter is less extreme, this may very well be all you ever need for the rare

occasions you camp in the winter. The even better news: in some regions, lean-tos offer a place to camp along the trail that will be largely sheltered from the elements. If you're able to plan your camping excursion around such a site (or, in more rare cases, a backwoods hut or lodge, such as the AMC hut network in New Hampshire's White Mountains), a lot of the worry about the wind and snow bulldozing your tent should be mitigated.

Another approach, and one that should be strongly considered when you're first trying out cold weather camping for the first time, is to simply avoid camping when conditions are dangerously wintery. Winter does not always mean snow, and in most regions, snow is the exception rather than the rule even during the height of the winter months. The best way to learn about cold weather camping is to start when the temperature remains above freezing, and thus, when many of the dangers of winter are reasonably mitigated. You'll be more comfortable, and you'll feel safer.

But let's assume that you can't find a lean-to or hut, and are planning to set up camp at an open clearing near the summit of your mountain-tackling hike. Let's assume, too, this a relatively moderate hike—you probably shouldn't be camping in places like the Rocky Mountains in winter until you've accumulated years of real-world experience in all types of terrain and weather conditions. To start out, how might you go about preparing your tent for a winter hike?

Winter tents are engineered to hold up to extreme weather conditions, even in alpine environments where there's little to buffer the full force of the wind. This is truly the most dangerous and intense variety of camping, but you can drop the challenge level several notches if you're able to camp below the tree line, where the impact of the wind will be buffered by the trees. With this sort of reliable shelter and shade, there's also less chance of snowfall piling up around your tent throughout the night. This is the only truly safe course of action if you are camping using a three-season tent, especially in an area like New York's Adirondacks or New Hampshire's White Mountains, and even more so in the greater mountains of the West Coast, where conditions can be especially brutal above the tree line.

Before setting out, there's one more way your three-season tent might let you down, but it's easy to discover in advance. Find out what kind of material your tent poles are made out of—ideally, they'll be aluminum or carbon fiber, rather than fiberglass. Aluminum tent poles and trekking poles are strong enough to use in cold weather and should hold up to the additional pressure from modest layers of snow on the roof of the tent, but fiberglass tent poles will sometimes shatter in freezing temperatures when placed under stress. Wet snow is extremely heavy, and even a few inches of snow can be enough to cave in a tent using fiberglass tent poles.

Selecting a Camp Site

Finding a good campsite in the winter is simpler in many ways. The ground is free of brush, and with a blanket of snow, essentially all good tent sites will be flat and easy to set up upon. Nonetheless, you will also want to be a good deal more selective than you typically would be in the warm-weather months. Setting up camp in an area with its own natural shelter is the best way to avoid snow unexpectedly piling up and wind aggressively tearing through. Again, if you are using a 3-season tent to camp in the winter, you'll want to look for a spot below the tree line, preferably in a col (the saddle or ridge between two adjacent mountain summits) or a rocky low point where the mountains themselves will help to block the wind. Every tent has its limits, and no matter how sturdy or well-designed your tent may be, it's going to be in danger of collapsing if there's too much snow piled upon it.

Exactly how much snow your tent can handle will depend on its particular design, of course. Tents

Opposite: Finding flat ground for your tent can be easier in the winter with snow on the ground, but you'll need to search for cover from the wind and snow as well, particularly in mountainous areas.

with a steeper roofline will shed snow better, but tents designed specifically for winter camping will also have stronger poles and a structure engineered to hold up to additional weight. Whichever tent you own, keep in mind that you may have to periodically push against the roof of your tent in the middle of the night to "punch" snow away if it begins to accumulate rapidly. As annoying as this may be, it's certainly preferable to your tent collapsing because too much snow accumulated above you.

Finally, there's one more trick you can use to keep snow and wind from compromising your tent. Backpackers already know to pack a tarp or tent footprint to provide an additional buffer between the ground and the actual bottom of your tent. Pitching your tent directly onto the ground—especially onto snowy ground—is an invitation for a wet, cold, soggy floor. In winter, you may wish to pack a second tarp for your camping adventures, which can be set up like a shield between your tent and the wind, or even above your tent, to prevent snow from falling onto the tent in the first place. If you don't end up actually needing your tarp for cover, you can always lay it out as an additional footprint between the bottom of your tent and the ground. Two tarps between your tent and the snow-covered earth simply means extra protection between you and the frigid outside world.

Securing Your Tent

You'll need to be sure your tent remains secure throughout the night, which is considerably more difficult on snowy ground than on hard soil. Standard tent stakes are designed for solid earth, not snow and ice. While dirt is compact enough to hold a thin metal stake in place, snow is of course much

looser, and a strong wind will often be enough to pry your stakes out, leaving your tent unsecured. Fortunately, you can use the malleable nature of snow to your advantage here.

One of the easiest ways to modify your tent's anchoring system for the winter is to find a short but hefty stick and tie a guyline to it, then bury the stick in the snow. As the stick is more substantial than a metal stake, and has far more surface texture, it should remain in place as the snow hardens and freezes overnight. This is called a deadman, and many other household items can be put to the task as well. Plastic grocery bags can serve this function quite well, as you can simply stuff them full of snow, tie your guylines to the handles, and then bury them. But if you're a gearhead that likes to always have the exact right tool for every job, snow stakes designed for this particular challenge are available through many outfitters.

Sleeping Bags

Once you're confident that you've got a tent that can hold up to the weather—and that you'll be able to set up camp where the worst of the weather is neutralized by your environment—you'll need to focus on staying warm. Your tent, after all, is mostly there to keep the elements out, but three-season tents are designed for ventilation, rather than retaining warmth. In order to stay warm, you'll be relying primarily on your sleeping bag and camp clothes. Indeed, when buying a sleeping bag, the key variable between bags is the temperature rating. Some bags are lighter in weight and pack down better than others, but this also corresponds to their insulating properties. As with tents, three-season sleeping bags are the default,

When camping in the winter, finding a location with a lean-to will go a long way in mitigating the shortcomings of a three-season tent.

Winter camping necessitates packing a significant amount of extra gear and clothing, and thus demands extreme preparation and precautions.

though more specialized bags are available as well, including sleeping bags designed specifically with winter camping in mind.

The temperature ratings for sleeping bags are not the most precise figures, to be sure. Everyone's body and comfort levels are different, so no single rating could possibly apply perfectly across the spectrum of humanity. Temperature ratings should rather be viewed as a general metric—you'll have to fine-tune your comfort level in the moment based on weather conditions and your own preferences. This, at least, has gotten somewhat easier in recent years. Before 2005, there was no standardized rating system for sleeping bag temperatures, and manufacturers' ratings could vary wildly depending on their particular methods. Customers might often find themselves playing a guessing game to figure out whether a bag from a new manufacturer would hold up to real world use. Eventually, the EN (European Norm) Standard was introduced, ensuring that sleeping bags were independently tested and provided with a comfort and limit rating. In 2017, the EN rating system was further updated with the current ISO standard, adding even more consistency.

A bag's ***comfort rating*** is geared toward campers who tend to feel chilled more easily, meaning that this number will err on the side of caution. This temperature rating is typically the one that brands will highlight on women's bags, due to women often having a lower metabolic rate than men. A ***lower limit rating*** skews the opposite direction and is therefore always lower than the comfort rating. This is the temperature rating brands use on men's bags and indicates the temperature at which a warm sleeper (someone with a higher metabolic rate) might still feel comfortable. Obviously, such ratings cannot be universal. Whoever you are, and however you identify, if you tend to feel cold easily, stick with the comfort rating. If you tend to run hot, then stick with the lower limit rating.

The temperature referenced in the advertised name of the bag is often simply a rounded-up or rounded-down marketing number, but the bag's specifications should give you its precise rating. In spring, summer, and fall, this slight discrepancy may not matter much, but a difference of only a few degrees can result in a significant amount of discomfort under winter conditions. Brands will typically round up or down to a number that ends in a 0 or a 5, and so a bag sold as the "Snuggypile 20," for instance, might have a lower limit rating of 23°F. There are no rules about whether a manufacturer can round up or round down, but again, the exact rating should be given in the item's specifications.

One more quirk of winter sleeping bags that's worth noting: since women's bags err toward the more conservative temperature rating, at a given temperature, women's bags often weigh more than men's bags even with the same temp rating. This is due to women's bags using the more conservative comfort rating, which requires additional insulation compared to another bag's looser (cooler) lower limit rating. Finally, not every bag on the market will have an EN or ISO rating. Manufacturers will often not go to the trouble of testing and rating bags intended for more casual camping use, and children's bags often skip these ratings as well. Any sleeping bag intended only for casual camping should never be used in winter conditions, so if you can't find any information on the bag's temperature limits, it's probably better not to use it.

While the EN/ISO protocols ensure that rating tests are conducted with the same benchmarks from brand to brand, they obviously can't account for what clothing you wear to bed, what gear you're using (such as sleeping pads and various tent set-ups), differences in body type and metabolism, varying weather conditions across our country's great range of climates, what you ate and when you ate dinner, and so on. So, when it comes time to use your sleeping bag in the wild, its comfort level will almost certainly differ from its tested temperature rating. If you packed well with a range of clothing options, however, you should be able to adjust your layers accordingly, adding or dissipating warmth as needed.

Sleeping Pads

A sleeping pad serves as the main buffer between you and the cold ground, and without one, even a top of the line sleeping bag may fail to keep you warm all night. That's to say nothing of your comfort—in my experience, nothing guarantees a night of fitful unrest like trying to sleep on a lumpy, hard surface. As someone who doesn't sleep well when camping even under the best of circumstances, I usually bring two sleeping pads whenever I can: a basic foam sleeping pad that rolls up and can be strapped to the back of my pack, and an inflating pad, which by default has more cushioning and usually holds a better insulation value as well.

Basic foam pads are usually little more than a sheet of foam, and are thus lightweight, inexpensive, and very durable. You won't need to worry about punctures or leaks, and these pads work great beneath other, better insulated pads, as they'll spare your fancier inflating pads from punctures and go a long way to buffer against the cold ground. Their bulky rolled-up or folded shape also makes them convenient to sit on when breaking for lunch or making camp. Unless you are a particularly good sleeper—someone with the magic ability to pass out quickly regardless of your comfort level—I would not recommend relying exclusively upon this type of pad, though there's little reason to not carry one with you, given how little they weigh.

Other types of sleeping pads get a bit more complicated. Here, again, you'll want to pay close attention to temperature ratings: sleeping pads are designated with an R-value, which indicates resistance to heat flow. The higher a pad's R-value, the more insulation from the cold ground it will offer. Sleeping pad R-values range from less than 2 (minimal insulation) to 5.5 or higher (very insulated). As with sleeping bags, the R-value protocol is standardized, so these values hold the same meaning from brand to brand. The scale is also stackable, so that if you're layering multiple pads on top of one another, some simple math will give you an idea of how much insulation they'll provide. A pad with an R-value of 4.0 is twice as warm as pad with an R-value of 2.0, and two pads with an R-value of 2.0 stacked on top of each other should be roughly the equivalent of a single pad with an R-value of 4.0.

Extra Clothing

Regardless of any other factors, you will, without a doubt, require additional insulation layers when camping in winter. The clothing you wear on a typical winter hike is, for the most part, designed to guard against extremes and the cold that slinks in whenever you stop for a break. Camping is basically taking a very, very long break, so to speak, and doing so during the coldest portion of the day, so the standard insulation layers that you'd typically pack won't be enough. This is especially true if you'll be camping in a 3-season tent or camping in temperatures that push the threshold of your sleeping bag's temperature rating.

If you don't wear long underwear when hiking, you'll almost certainly need it once you make camp, and you'll be a whole lot more comfortable sleeping at night wearing it as well.

Fortifying Your Camp

Light snow shovels or avalanche shovels can serve multiple functions when camping in the winter. Avalanche shovels are designed for emergency situations when an avalanche occurs—more on that in chapter 7. However, these shovels are more frequently used for modifying your campsite. If the snow around you has drifted, it may be helpful to shape a platform on which to pitch your tent. But if you are using a 3-season tent, or camping in a particularly windy area, a snow shovel will also be useful for creating snow "fortifications" around your tent, blocking the wind in places where your tent may be particularly drafty.

Most tents have a rain fly to cover the vestibule area, but these coverings are not designed with winter in mind. Remember, most three-season tents seek to maximize their ventilation, which makes them extremely ineffective at retaining warmth in the winter. The vestibule area often leaves a big air gap at ground level, and this can leave a serious opening for wind to rush right into your tent. You can prevent this by using a shovel to pile snow around the base of your tent like a low wall. Doing this doesn't demand a lot of time or effort but can make a big difference.

Drinking Water Safety

Finding water when you're camping usually doesn't require a whole lot of thought—you just look at your map and ensure you'll be passing by, or ide-

Accessing water in the winter can be difficult, as the edges of ponds and streams often freeze, making it unclear where solid ground begins and ends.

ally camping next to, a water source. In winter, things become a bit more difficult, but by honing your winter intuition, you should at least be able to narrow your expectations and reduce the number of contingency options you'll need. If you are going to be hiking and camping in a region that has seen sub-freezing temperatures for an extended period of time, even a fast-running stream might be frozen over. Under such circumstances, you'll probably have an easier time melting snow than finding liquid water, but this invites complications of its own. Melting snow in order to replenish your water supply and cook your meals will use up a lot of fuel—make sure the fuel canister for your camp stove isn't about to run out!—and will also necessitate a lot of time breaking down and unpacking your gear.

Though it might seem an easy solution to winter's water conundrum, never eat snow. While there isn't necessarily anything wrong with the quality of pristine wilderness snow itself, snow is obviously rather cold, and that itself is no good. Cold snow entering your stomach will lower your body's core temperature. Unless you have absolutely no other options, don't consume snow until it's been melted into water.

Additionally, no matter where you get your water from in the wild, you will need a reliable method of purification or pasteurization. Even frigid winter temperatures are not enough to curb parasites like *Giardia lamblia* that are frequently found in wild water sources. These harmful microbes are so common that all water from natural sources must be filtered or sterilized before drinking. Boiling will do the trick, but as discussed above, boiling all of your drinking water requires a lot of fuel, time, and effort. Most hikers simply use a specialty water filter, regardless of the season. In both the

summer and winter, a water filter is the easiest, most effective, and best-tasting option. While there are numerous styles of filter available at nearly all outdoor outfitters, I personally prefer a simple pump-action filter.

The next challenge is actually finding liquid water. Tracking it down can be difficult, and even simply accessing it can pose significant dangers. Nonetheless, in most areas, there are often streams and creeks that run throughout winter. How reliable these may be will depend entirely on where you are located: if temperatures have remained below freezing for long stretches of time, most streams may be frozen over, or hidden by snow. If temperatures have swung back and forth, however, you'll likely have an easier time finding running water. Often, it simply makes the most sense to plan any camping expeditions based around where you know you'll be able to find water by first surveying a detailed topographical map, rather than wasting hours in attempts to uncover it by chance.

When you do find water, safe access is key. Most ponds and lakes only freeze over under persistent, extreme winter conditions, but even then, the crust of ice is only so thick. A little digging or drilling will be enough to crack through the ice of a frozen pond or semi-frozen creek to access running water, but this task should be approached with care. Likewise, when accessing water from a stream or creek, drifts of snow make deciphering the edges of the water quite difficult, and before you know it, you might find yourself stepping knee-deep in ice-cold water, or even worse, tripping and dunking your whole body in a frigid stream. Such a scenario can be extremely dangerous and should be met with caution.

Whether you're trying to access a stream, creek, or pond, prod with your hiking poles to test out each step, and scrape away snow as necessary to see if you can expose liquid water beneath. Always take tentative steps forward, without putting your entire body weight on your front foot. If you explore cautiously, you should be able to sense when you've left the security of solid ground. An ice axe will come in especially useful here, as it can be used both to prod the ground ahead of you, and to dig a hole through a sheet of ice as well. If you've found an opening to liquid water but don't feel you can safely stand above it without breaking through the ice or snow, try lowering a bottle into the water using string or twine and a hiking pole as leverage, so that you're able to stand back on stable ground.

Cooking Safety

If you are camping in an area where there's significant snowfall, chances are that any bears should be hibernating for the winter. Nonetheless, it's always good to play things safe and tie your food up hanging from a tree limb at least a hundred feet from your camp. A bear canister will serve the same purpose, but these are heavy to carry and may not be necessary in the winter. Still, critters other than bears will be interested in your food as well, and many animals are still active throughout the winter months, regardless of snow. Always make sure your food is securely stashed away and placed out of reach for the night.

Opposite: While potentially dangerous, frozen rivers and streams can make for a mesmerizing sight.

Campfires in Winter

There is something mesmerizing about fire, the hypnotic dance of a flickering flame. Winter, unsurprisingly, draws us to fire more than any other time of year. So many of our indoor winter traditions are centered around fire. There's of course the fireplace, though slightly out of fashion these days, which has simply been replaced by smaller, more manageable fires in the form of candles (a multi-billion-dollar business in America today). Most of us prefer to keep our fires indoors in the winter, of course. Even with the warmth inherent in a fire, sitting still for so long outside in the winter is more than most of us want to endure, at least when we have the comforts of our living room close at hand. In the wilderness, of course, it's a different story. When camping in the winter, it's nearly a must. For both practical and mystical reasons, the allure of the campfire is all the more appealing in the snow.

Even in winter, you'll need to practice fire safety principles. A forest fire is equally as damaging no matter the season of the year. Even with snow on the ground, always make sure your campfire is extinguished before going to bed or leaving the area. With that said, actually starting a fire in winter can be a bit more of a challenge. While downed wood should be easy to find, chances are it may not be dry.

First, collect tinder. Dry birch bark, twigs, and dead and dry pine needles make for good tinder. If you are hiking into an area where such fuel may be scarce or difficult to locate, it's not a bad idea to collect tinder as you hike and pack it away in a bag. Along with tinder, you'll also want kindling, the small to medium size sticks that keep a fire going once you've gotten it lit, and help fuel the fire until it's strong enough to burn real firewood. Finally, you'll want wood that will burn clean for a long time, sustaining your fire. Dead branches roughly the size of your wrist or lower arm will work best, and the older and dryer the better.

When you've established your campsite, dig out a pit in the snow where you'll build your fire. A pit about two feet across works well so that the surrounding snow doesn't melt into the fire. If you can find stones or small rocks, place them around the pit to designate a fire ring. Now, you'll have to lay down a foundation, or your fire will simply melt the snow beneath it and extinguish itself. A few large flat rocks will serve, if you can find them, or else you can use several thick branches.

Place a handful of tinder in the center of the fire-pit foundation and build a "teepee" around this with pieces of kindling. To start with, keep this structure simple, using only a few pieces of wood. This will concentrate the heat while also enabling sufficient airflow. Always play it safe when starting a campfire, even in winter. While the snow-covered ground may seem as if it would automatically prevent a forest fire, keep in mind that there's a lot of downed dead wood laying around in this season as well. Practice an abundance of caution when making campfires in the woods, and never use flammable fluids to stoke a fire. Dry old birch bark is particularly effective as a fire starter, but if conditions are wet or windy, you can always pack a commercial fire starter as a backup or pack some homemade fire starter. Dryer lint works very well, as do cotton balls dipped in Vaseline.

Once the tinder is burning, begin to layer additional pieces of kindling around the teepee. Remember that fires need oxygen, so don't overcrowd your fire. Extra wood won't help if your

Campfires are practically a must when camping in the winter, but wilderness fire safety protocols should still be followed.

fire runs out of air first. Once the fire is burning strongly, place a piece of firewood next to the kindling so that the fire may begin to spread. Continue adding wood as needed so that your fire burns at a steady pace. Because it will likely be surrounded by snow, you won't want to build it up too big. Large campfires are both a fire hazard and, in winter, can sometimes put themselves out if they melt the snow surrounding them too quickly. And as always, even if your fire is surrounded by frozen water, be sure that it's entirely extinguished before you go to bed.

Other Tips and Tricks

As circumstantial as winter hiking ultimately is, there are a few clever tricks that hikers and campers have devised that can make a big difference under a number of circumstances. In winter, many hikers prefer to carry their water in a stainless-steel thermos, otherwise known as a vacuum flask, since such a vessel will help to prevent your water from immediately freezing. When camping, you'll want to pack a camp stove for preparing both food and beverages. In the evening, after brewing up some tea or hot cocoa, leave your camp stove out and fill it with snow (which will begin to melt so long as the metal remains warm). Once you're almost done with your beverage, fire up the stove and melt enough snow to refill your thermos most of the way to the top. Seal it tightly, or you'll risk burning yourself by jostling the bottle in the night. You can probably see where this is going: your thermos, full of hot water, will retain that heat for a long time. As long as it's well sealed and isn't in danger of leaking, you can tuck the bottle into your sleep bag—down by your feet is best—and benefit from the trickle of warmth it'll give off throughout the night.

Cleaning up camp and prepping for bed will hopefully help you to warm up before you crawl into your tent, but if you're still feeling chilled by the time you're ready to sleep, spending a few minutes doing a light exercise like sit-ups can help to generate body heat. A quick change of clothes will also go a long way in ensuring your comfort.

Opposite: Dusk in the backcountry with a fresh blanket of snow on the ground can make for one of the most beautiful scenes a hiker will ever experience.

Snow is as complex as it is beautiful.

6.

UNDERSTANDING SNOW

Snowflakes embody both simplicity and uniqueness. A single snowflake is as unique as a fingerprint, but enough of them piled together become a uniform blanket to our eyes. Yet even when snow accumulates in big bland piles, it's a surprisingly complicated phenomenon.

Did you know that the ice we commonly encounter on a regular basis is only one of at least eighteen possible phases of ice? What we think of as ice is designated as "ice Ih" or ice-phase-one, but there are a multitude of other varieties of ice to be found throughout the extreme conditions of the universe. Ice forms via numerous different phases, or packing geometries, as a result of variations in temperature and pressure. Fortunately, for the purposes of winter hiking, we only need to concern ourselves with good old ice 1h in its classic hexagonal crystalline structure—unless you're planning to go hiking somewhere out in deep space (which, admittedly, does sound pretty fun). Still, it's worth noting that pressure, and not just temperature, plays a major role in the formation and structure of ice. Back here on Earth, however, the shifting structure of a snowpack is also heavily influenced by both temperature and pressure, and these factors will have a significant impact on the sort of experience you'll find out on the trail.

Almost anyone who lives in a wintry region has, at some point in their life, experienced a total wipeout on a compacted snowy surface that turned out to be as slick as an ice rink. The various stages of the changing snowpack represent unique challenges and dangers to us hikers (as well as simple joys, for those who have not lost their youthful wonder). A difference of only a degree above or a degree below freezing can have a huge impact on the type of snow

that falls. From fine, dry powder to sopping wet slush, sleet-like ice to hard, sand-like grains, the many varieties of snow are all the result of slight variations in moisture and air temperature, both miles above at cloud level or close to the ground.

Understanding how snowpack changes due to temperature and pressure variations will help you to develop better intuition for how conditions on the trail will progress over time. Monitoring the weather is only part of the equation, as snow is a highly dynamic substance, and thus conditions in the wild can change dramatically literally overnight.

What Causes Snow?

There are plenty of factors that go into snow formation, but even the tiniest changes in weather can turn what would have been chilly rain into a snowstorm. Air temperature is probably the most obvious primary variable, and small fluctuations in the atmosphere are highly influential, though often too slight or remote for a human to notice. Minor changes in temperature around the freezing point can make a huge difference not only in terms of snow forming, but in the consistency of the snow that does form.

Humidity also plays a role, and while we might be able to easily discern the difference between very high humidity and very low humidity, the range of moisture levels between these extremes is harder to parse. Moisture content will generally be higher in maritime climates where the air temperature is warmer, while in colder regions, like

Large mountains often create their own weather patterns, attracting snow due to both their elevation and the disruptions they cause to atmospheric air currents.

the northeastern United States, winters tend to be dryer. Of course, as the climate changes, rapid shifts in weather are happening more and more frequently, and such inconsistencies are perhaps even more noticeable in winter than during other seasons. But even under the best of circumstances weather can be difficult to predict, and a generally dry winter in a region like the northeast can still produce slushy snow on a day with greater than average humidity.

Particular geographic regions will often receive more snow than others, even when those regions are adjacent to each other. Being that a great deal of hiking is done in mountainous areas, it's worth noting that snow and mountains have a special relationship with one another. Mountains generate or attract snow, while low-lying regions generally do not. Even in an area where the mountains are only a few thousand feet higher in elevation, you'll reliably find more snow up on the summits than in the foothills. Why is this?

Snow forms high up in the atmosphere. We seldom stop to consider just how divergent conditions at high elevation are from conditions down on the ground. Snow forms in clouds that are below freezing, and temperatures in mountain atmospheres can drop below freezing throughout the year, not only in winter. When temperatures in the mountains are cold enough, moisture is usually drawn to the summits in the form of snow. Consider this: much of the rain that falls in the spring and autumn actually starts out as snow, and simply melts long before we can see it as such. So mountains, being intermediaries between the earth and the sky, get blessed with more snow as a result of their elevation and unique weather patterns. Even a small chain of mountains can create what's called a rain shadow effect. Essentially, mountains serve as a barrier for saturated air blowing inland, drawing precipitation out of the air and literally blocking it from reaching the low-lying regions beyond. This is why the Pacific Northwest is generally wet and rainy, while regions due east of the Rocky Mountains are dry and arid.

Wet and Dry Snow

Wet snow is the result of temperatures hovering just around the freezing point or slightly above, partially but not fully melting the snow as it drifts through the sky. Snowflakes that remained below freezing as they formed and fell to the earth will be smaller and drier, and won't stick to other snowflakes as easily. Dry, powdery snow is common on high mountain peaks, where the temperatures are consistently below freezing. Fortunately, this is just the sort of snow that is ideal for skiers. Down in the suburbs, snow is more likely to have gone through a period of partial melting, but such heavy, wet snow is just the sort that children delight in, as it's perfect for snowball fights and sculpting snowmen.

As a general rule, snow crystals fall with their broad surfaces roughly horizontal, much like a parachute. Drifting downward through the air, they rotate, and as their edges are in contact with the most water vapor, the growth of snow crystals occurs primarily from those edges. This results in the many unique shapes that snowflakes are known for. If a snowflake passes through a layer of supercooled droplets while falling, it will become coated with rime. If enough droplets coat a crystal it becomes what is known as graupel, a small lump of snow crystal so heavily rimed that the underlying snowflake is trapped within. An accumulation of dry, light snow can be thought of more as a froth of air and ice whipped together than as a solid mass. Much like foam on top of a cappuccino, it is

A snowstorm blows down from the mountains and through the valley below at Wyoming's Grand Teton National Park.

a beautiful, delicate, but fairly unstable substance that can either disperse or condense into a more stable form.

Since snow is of great interest to so many different groups of people, from meteorologists to avid skiers to a variety of northern cultures around the world, there are a shocking number of different terms for the various forms of snowfall—from "blue" and "Colorado super chunk" to "poo ice" and "zastrugi." As hikers, however, we are mostly concerned with the properties of snow on the ground, and the changes the snowpack experiences over time.

The Ever-Changing Snowpack

As anyone who lives in a northern climate can attest, a blanket of snow will change quite drastically before eventually melting away. As a general rule, the more variation in temperature and weather, the greater the changes the snowpack will endure. Snow is strange stuff even in its most basic form, with numerous properties that cause it to behave unlike any other natural substance you're likely to encounter out in the wild.

Fresh snow has a very low density due to the fact that freshly accumulated snow is mostly air. Yet it is

Understanding how the snowpack changes with time, temperature, and pressure is vital to building an intuition for conditions out on the trail.

The snowpack on high-altitude mountains will usually be far more complex than in low-lying areas due to the volume of snow accumulated over the course of the winter season.

also a highly effective insulator—as demonstrated by the fact that people can live comfortably inside an igloo. But one way or another, every pristine, gorgeous blanket of fresh snow will inevitably become compacted and grow denser, and this progression creates conditions that any winter adventurer will need to be mindful of. Even as fresh snow continues to pile up, the weight of the upper layers will eventually compact the lower layers, transforming those lower layers into something much denser than the snow most of us are used to. In many regions, rising temperatures will disperse the snowpack before it becomes deep enough that such accumulation will be possible, though some mountainous areas host conditions that can generate truly mind-boggling amounts of snow. In the Cascade Mountains of Washington State, several historic winter seasons registered accumulations of nearly 100 feet of snow—nearly enough to bury an entire ten-story building.

If such snow depth sounds beyond comprehension, remember that much of North America was once covered by glaciers a mile thick. The ice at the bottom of such glaciers is quite unlike the sort of ice you'll find in your backyard in winter. These glaciers reshaped the entire landscape, carving out mountains and valleys much like ocean waves sculpting the sand. We may take snow for granted, but it truly is one of the most fascinating substances on the planet—at times so low in density that children can lob missiles of the stuff without any fear of harm, and yet holding the potential to transform into a destructive force so potent, it can bulldoze entire mountains and reshape the Earth in ways that are observable for millions of years.

Snow evolves as it forms, as it falls, and continues to change regularly after landing. As a general rule, the larger the flakes of snow, the more loosely they will nestle against each other, and the more quickly the resulting snowpack will change.

Any niche subject can be expected to birth its own complex terminology, and the study of snow and glaciers is no different. "Sintering," for example, is the process that occurs when snow crystals lose their points due to molecular motion, wind, or direct pressure, and reform into larger, denser grains. Simply physically breaking up snow crystals is sintering, and thus sintering happens whenever we walk on or shovel snow. Melting and other forces of friction can cause sintering as well. After the crystalline arms of the snowflakes are broken, the remaining grains fuse, forming and freezing into larger crystals. At the ultimate stage of snowpack metamorphism, a hardened form of snow called "firn" transitions into glacial ice. At this stage, what once was snow will have compacted into a form resembling glass.

Why Sintering Matters to Hikers

Since only a few regions of the country are consistently cold enough to sustain thick layers of deep snow, most of us will only ever observe a fast-paced, dramatically shifting snowpack, rather than the slower, more dramatic evolution of firn and glacial ice. Nonetheless, even a short-lived snowpack can be quite dynamic, and many of the changes will have an impact on the exact gear you'll need for your hike. Because sintering can result from com-

pression like constant footsteps, it is the reason why dense, hard ice stubbornly clings to popular hiking trails well after the rest of the snowpack has melted from the surrounding landscape. This is also why packed-down hiking trails so quickly become hard and slick, and dangerous to walk upon without traction devices. The more compressed the snow, the less it resembles its original "froth" state, and the more it begins to mimic a layer of solid ice.

Ice can form quickly, even on top of a snowpack that was fresh and dry and powdery only a few days before. Usually, a sintered layer of snow is thin enough that your boots will crack through easily, punching a hole through the ice and into the softer snow below, rather than skidding. However, over the course of an entire season with frequent thaw and freeze cycles, the entire snowpack can eventually become just as dense, and far more challenging to traverse.

Snow becomes denser and harder as sintering progresses, which is called "settlement." Skiers and other alpine adventurers will sometimes refer to the sudden collapse of a snowpack as "settling," but as a technical term, settlement specifically refers to a gradual process. The sudden collapse of a snowpack, which can signify the start of an avalanche (and which is therefore something all skiers need to be alert to), creates a deep, resonate "whumpf" sound. Funnily enough, "whumpfing" is indeed the technical term for this sort of rapid, sudden snowpack collapse.

Settling happens faster at warmer temperatures (resulting in wet snow) than in colder temperatures (which creates dry, powdery snow, prone to drifting easily in the wind). When new snow settles, it forms cones around trees and poles and other obstacles. The snow bonds to the tree, and this bond props up the snow like a pole props up a tent.

Winter weather is notoriously unpredictable, and you should always be prepared for a sudden snowstorm—even in the desert.

The more dramatic and rapid the changes in weather, the more the snowpack itself will change, but the repeated movement of humans across a hiking trail compounds these effects even more. Trails that see consistent traffic and regular snowfall throughout the winter are likely to be packed down to the point that the snow will have been compressed into hard, treacherous ice.

Fresh or recent snow can always provide a new layer of traction, but by the end of winter, any popular trail that does not receive direct sunlight is likely to be quite difficult to traverse without traction devices. Icy conditions may linger on such trails for many days, even weeks, after snow has vanished from the surrounding landscape. At lower elevations, rising spring temps may melt this ice relatively quickly, but if you plan to head into the mountains, don't be surprised to encounter such conditions long after snow is a distant memory in low-lying areas.

Where I live in New York, I expect to encounter packed-down, icy trail conditions in the Catskill Mountains for at least a month after the last period of consistent snowfall and freezing temps. Again, elevation and exposure to sunlight make a huge difference. Even in the mountains, ice may linger on one side of the mountain for weeks after it's all-but-gone on the other side of the slope—and if the trail circles the mountain, you should expect to possibly encounter all sorts of conditions from one mile to the next. Given the low angle of the sun in winter, it's virtually assured that no two sides of a mountain will host the same conditions.

Needle Ice

Having a general awareness of the forces that shape and reshape a snowpack over the season is useful for developing your instincts, helping you to anticipate the sorts of conditions you might encounter across the trail. While this information is useful, it does not always cast the winter season in the most flattering light. Ice layers above and below the snowpack make for treacherous footing, and those last lingering sheets of mud-ice that we hike across in the spring are hardly nature's most flattering features. Still, the transformations of snow and ice across the weather spectrum can also lead to some truly marvelous sights. Some, like the phenomenon of needle ice, appear so unlikely and so strange, it's difficult to imagine how even the wild forces of nature could conspire to create them.

You've probably observed needle ice before, even if you didn't know what it was called. It's small and easily missed—though under optimal conditions, it has been known to grow as long as a foot—and tends to form in small muddy divots alongside the trail, or where the forest floor has been disturbed. It has a filamentous appearance, which means that it forms as clusters of needles, almost like a strange fractal geode one might find in a cavern. There are many other colloquial names for the phenomenon that speak to its strange appearance: frost flowers, ice castles, ice fringes, comb ice, ice flowers, and ice ribbons.

Despite their apparent oddity, the physics behind the formation of needle ice is actually well understood and relatively straightforward. The first requirement for the creation of ice needles is the presence of flowing groundwater that comes into contact with cold, sub-freezing air. Continued hydrostatic pressure from the ground water forces the ice upward into the air even after freezing has occurred, growing the columns of ice like a stalagmite in a cave. This continued, pressure-fed growth

results in the long, extruded shapes that needle ice is known for. Needle ice cannot form just anywhere, of course, but the conditions on the side of hills and mountains are often ideal. Seeping groundwater is usually found on highly sloped ground, ensuring the necessary hydrostatic pressure. Since needle ice does require running water in order to form, look for it during periods where the temperature dips above and below freezing, especially at night. It's usually small and easy to miss, but once you begin to notice it, you may start to see needle ice on a regular basis in the winter.

White Mountains, New Hampshire

7.

WINTER WEATHER AND OTHER HAZARDS

Weather in winter is a different sort of creature than the squalls of spring and summer, there's no denying that. Winter poses risks that are simply more persistent and more challenging to avoid than any other season. Yes, the dangers are there—but they are also manageable. Most of them can be navigated by merely calling upon a heightened common sense, just as one would approach the dangers of summer. A standard hiking guide doesn't need to go out of its way to warn you about the peril of a fluke thunderstorm in June, since you probably already instinctively avoid lightning. Winter's dangers, being somewhat more obscure and less frequently discussed, do require just that sort of elaboration. But this should not suggest that the winter landscape is insurmountable. What it should suggest, instead, is that there is simply a new base of knowledge that you'll have to develop first.

Some of the sections in this chapter cover material that will perhaps intimidate you, and might even give you anxiety. But don't panic, and definitely don't avoid this chapter. Better to have all the information available and yet never need it than to run headfirst into danger whilst ignorant, right? Winter poses many dangers, but these dangers can be easily managed with the appropriate attention and preparation. Unlike the sorts of accidents that might occur while we're driving our car or crossing the street in the city, the threats posed to us by nature are largely predictable, at least with adequate research, intuition, and foresight.

On most hikes, temperature and trail conditions are the primary factors that a hiker should concern themselves with, but they're certainly not the only threats that winter can offer up. Ice, storms, whiteouts, fragile ice shelves, spruce traps, and avalanches are just a few of the dangers that come along with winter adventuring. Nonetheless, you can avoid almost all of these hazards if you learn what they are, where and why they're likely to occur, and how to stay away from them.

Falling Ice

While this may seem one of the more common-sense winter hazards to watch out for, and perhaps the easiest to avoid by simply paying attention, falling ice truly can be incredibly dangerous. Mountainous areas with steep cliffs and overhangs can drop projectiles on you out of nowhere, and a sufficiently heavy or sharp bit of ice will do a lot of damage. In the winter, in the backwoods, even a minor injury must be taken seriously, and the harm done by a large piece of ice could even prove fatal. Always practice extra caution when traveling around the underside of cliffs. In a dense forest, such rock outcrops may be hidden from below, so as always, familiarize yourself with the terrain beforehand and always scan your surroundings thoroughly when entering a new area. If the weather is warm, or ice has formed in a spot where sunlight can strike it directly, ice formations may be extra fragile.

Undercut Snow

A thick blanket of snow can hide many obstacles—from rocks to broken branches to hidden streams of water. Running water, whether from an actual hidden stream or merely a trickle of snowmelt hugging the ground, can carve out channels beneath the snow. This can happen anywhere where gravity collects streams of water, but it's especially likely in valleys and in other low areas. This is especially a concern when attempting to find a water source, as you're by definition going to be venturing out to areas where water will have carved out channels below the snow. When navigating such places, probe ahead with your poles to test the stability of the snow before stepping on it. Wet clothing is perhaps the most mundane yet persistent danger of winter hiking, as it's a fast track to hypothermia. Avoid wet boots, socks, and pants at all costs.

Invisible Ice

Invisible ice, "black ice," or hidden ice isn't only an issue when driving in winter—though of course you'll need to watch out for it then too. Remember that compressed snow eventually becomes what we think of as ice, and that snow is in some sense just a variety of ice. Compressed snow does not need to "hide" ice to pose a risk, for compressed snow on its own can be every bit as slick and treacherous as a clear sheet of pure ice. Of course, snow can also quite literally hide ice, and you should be especially wary of this when there's a dusting of snow on the ground. More than a few inches of snow are usually enough to provide some traction, but a thin layer of powder may hide a ground layer of ice below it, and the slight dusting of snow isn't

Frozen waterfalls are one of winter's most beautiful sights, but don't get too close—falling ice can be extremely dangerous.

Ice forms more easily on rocky areas, and rocks themselves are more slick than solid earth. Always be extra vigilant and use traction gear when traversing rocky areas in the winter.

going to be enough to keep you on your feet. It's almost always best to wear spikes or other traction gear unless you're consistently trekking through firm, powdery snow.

Hidden Signs and Markers

Snow can hide more than ice—it can also hide the trail markers that you're counting on to find your way through the woods. The winter landscape is often disorienting enough as it is, particularly with fresh snow blown by the wind and coating the bark of trees. If such snow fell recently, trail markers become very easy to miss. If others have broken trail before you, however, this should be less of an issue—footprints, snowshoe tracks, and packed trails are generally easy to follow. But if you're the first to set out through a forest coated with virgin snow, be prepared to rely on your GPS and map-reading skills for navigation. If conditions are rough and you find yourself consistently losing the trail, consider how much time remains before sunset and at what point you will need to consider simply turning around. Remember that the trail back, at least, should not be nearly so difficult to follow, since your own path through the snow will be visible. It's always better to be safe than sorry, as the danger of becoming lost only increases after sunset.

Snow Blindness

Snow blindness is fairly self-explanatory, but it can really sneak up on you in the winter. The reflection off a solid snowpack truly can be dazzling, and not always in a good way. Fortunately, snow blindness is not actual blindness, and even a victim of serious snow blindness should recover with time. Still, if you're high up on a mountain in the snow, you probably don't want to wait too long before you're able to see again, and even temporarily snow blindness—becoming dazzled by the sheer intensity of the sun's reflecting light—can create serious problems. Whenever you'll be crossing large areas of snowpack, be sure to bring eye protection even if the forecast calls for a cloudy day. Sunglasses work fine for lower temperatures and more casual outings, but for more extreme environments, ski goggles are best.

Winter Storms

Winter storms can escalate quickly. While a thunderstorm in summer may send you unexpectedly scrambling to find shelter, such summer storms at least tend to blow through quickly. A winter storm, on the other hand, may leave you stranded and stuck even after it's long gone itself. Even once you push your way through the fresh snow and make it back to your car, travel on the newly dumped-upon roads may be an even greater issue. It's far too easy to get lost or injured in a blizzard. Your best bet is to take shelter from the wind where you can, and wait out the storm while staying warm, dry, and hydrated. Once you make it back to your car, you will at least have shelter there.

Whiteouts, though less common, go hand in hand with winter storms. With visibility reduced to almost nothing, a whiteout is an extremely dangerous situation for a hiker, especially if you're already high up on a mountain, where a few missteps can lead to serious injury. As disorienting and dangerous as a whiteout is, there are at least reliable ways to be on the lookout for them. Whiteouts generally require a wide-open space in order to occur, and are far more likely when the snow is fresh, dry, and easily blown about by the wind. Under such conditions, be extra vigilant for high winds, and consider backtracking to shelter before conditions deteriorate further. If there are any obvious landmarks around you, take note of them, as these can serve as guideposts if you become disoriented. If you are hiking down a trail where everything around you looks the same, and if the storm before you looks to be more than a passing squall, it may already be time to turn back.

The best way to combat this scenario is, of course, to avoid it. This may not sound like the most insightful advice in the world, but it really can't be stressed enough how crucial preparation is for ensuring a safe winter hike. Get into the habit of checking the weather repeatedly before an outing, and always check again before your departure, just in case the forecast has changed.

Secondly, leave a snow shovel in your vehicle. Many outdoor outfitters sell small, foldable shovels that can be easily (or somewhat easily) packed along when camping. Such a shovel won't take up much room in your car, and can be crucial for extracting your vehicle after an unexpected snowfall.

Frostbite

Despite the name, frostbite is essentially a burn. It occurs when flesh is exposed to a combination of cold, wind, and moisture, or when a person's extremities are subjected to extremely diminished circulation. Like the other common ailment of winter, hypothermia, frostbite is exacerbated by fatigue, lack of food, dampness, dehydration, and a lack of awareness on the part of the victim at the onset of the problem. Most common, mild occurrences of frostbite affect the cheeks, nose, or ears, as these are often the parts of the body most exposed to the elements. Your best protection against this variety of frostbite is a hat that can be pulled down over the ears, or a headband. Frostbite can also strike your fingers and toes if they are insufficiently protected as well. The best way to prevent this is basic awareness—watch out for that uncomfortable tingling feeling in your extremities—and make sure you have dry socks and a good, warm pair of gloves. It really is worth repeating: the best strategy for staying warm and safe on a winter adventure is to keep moving, and to set a pace so that you're generating comfortable levels of body heat.

It's very important to catch frostbite early. Frostbite is both dangerous and somewhat sneaky, as true frostbite itself is painless. As is also the case with hypothermia, the more severe it is, the less you'll feel it. The water in your flesh freezes, blood and oxygen cannot flow, and your nerve endings go numb. The affected extremities turn white and stiff as they literally freeze.

If you or someone in your party is suffering from advanced frostbite, you'll need to do what you can to restore circulation to the afflicted body part by gradually thawing it out. Don't rub or massage the affected area, however, as this can damage frozen flesh. A mild case of frostbite can be treated by rewarming the affected parts by holding them against warm skin, which is of course much easier if you're hiking in a group than solo. Unfortunately, thawing out a frostbitten appendage can be quite painful for the victim, and is of course not particularly comfortable for the person offering up their body heat either.

Thawing a case of mild frostbite will sometimes result in blisters, which should be treated like burn blisters. Treating severe frostbite while out in the wilderness is much more difficult, and again, every possible measure should be taken so that such a situation does not develop in the first place. Thaw-

Dangers like frostbite and hypothermia don't necessarily require extreme winter conditions, as wind and humidity are factors as well.

ing out advanced frostbite requires a long period constant warming. Under ideal conditions—which are likely impossible to arrange in a wilderness setting—the best approach is the immersion of the affected area in a warm water bath of a little more than 100°F. If you or anyone in your party has come down with frostbite that seems to be advancing beyond a very mild case, the best bet is to simply turn around and head back to your car. A serious instance of frostbite can leave lasting damage, and is much better dealt with by professionals in the emergency room, rather than hikers on a mountain trail.

Hypothermia

What happens when your body begins to lose too much heat? Heat loss occurs on what is essentially a sliding scale, and it is possible to feel slightly cold for many hours without putting yourself in any real danger, especially if you're moving and continuously generating warmth. If you find that you've begun regularly shivering, however, you need to start to pay attention.

The standard temperature of the human body is 98.6°F. When your body becomes too cold, dropping below this default temperature for a sustained

The best approach to hypothermia is to learn its signs and causes, and thus preempt it altogether.

period of time, its automatic response is to tighten and relax the muscles in rapid succession, generating warmth in an effort to restore itself to that ideal temperature. If your body drops below 95°F, however, shivering will become uncontrollable, and this is a sign that your body has crossed a dangerous threshold. You will begin to feel a numb tingling in your fingers and your toes, because your body has reduced blood flow to these regions in an effort to concentrate heat around your core. If uncontrollable shivering fails to halt the downward drop in your body temperature, the results can be extremely dangerous, and potentially fatal.

About a thousand people die from hypothermia in the United States every year. While I don't want to scare anyone off from venturing outside in the winter (more than five times that number choke to death every year, and this hopefully will not deter you from eating food) hypothermia really does need to be taken seriously. Much of this book, after all, is simply addressing the basic question: "How does one go outside in the winter without feeling too cold or putting oneself in danger?" Hypothermia being perhaps the chief of those dangers, it really is important to understand how it works in order to avoid it.

Hypothermia is not like an avalanche or a storm, where you can (theoretically, at least) check conditions ahead of time and attempt to avoid the situation entirely. Hypothermia can set in any time you venture outside in the cold—and though it may go against many people's intuition, the temperature doesn't have to be anywhere close to freezing for hypothermia to occur, so it's not simply a concern for winter hiking either. Damp, chilly weather—of the sort that's very common on the East Coast and in the Pacific Northwest—catches many people off-guard. Since hypothermia results from your body

temperature dropping below its stable baseline of 98.6°F, hypothermia is possible even in cool but not freezing air temperatures, particularly if your skin or clothing becomes wet. So while you should avoid excessive sweating, letting snow melt into your clothing, and should absolutely practice abundant caution when crossing streams, dehydration as well as malnourishment can also exacerbate hypothermia. If you're anything like me, you won't always feel particularly thirsty when hiking in the winter. Remind yourself to stay hydrated and well fed throughout your hike, even if you aren't craving refreshment.

Hypothermia can range from mild to severe cases. Mild hypothermia is actually fairly common, and many people experience it at some point in their lives. Mild hypothermia occurs when your core body temperature drops to about 95°F. Outdoorsy folks have coined a (perhaps unnecessarily) cute term for the symptoms of mild hypothermia: "the umbles." Most people at this stage begin mumbling, fumbling, and/or stumbling, on top of the shivering they've probably already been doing. These symptoms are a clear indicator that you need to be on your guard, and take steps to prevent hypothermia from advancing any further.

Mild Hypothermia

Below 95°F, things start to get a bit scarier. With every drop in degree below 95°F, your cerebral metabolic rate decreases by 3 to 5 percent. From 90°F to 94°F, most people begin to exhibit something like a mild form of amnesia, and may display a sudden indifference to their situation and the danger that they're in. Shivering kicks into high gear and becomes convulsive. Given this cognitive decline, someone's state of awareness can serve as a barometer of how badly hypothermia is affecting them. If they no longer even recognize that they're cold, mild hypothermia has likely turned into severe hypothermia.

Given that hypothermia often causes you to believe that there's nothing wrong, and that you aren't even cold at all, self-treatment can be difficult. If you are hiking alone and you're concerned that hypothermia may be setting in, it's best to practice an abundance of caution and address the situation before it worsens—if the situation escalates, you may not have the mental clarity to problem solve later.

If you or someone you're hiking with begins showing signs of mild hypothermia, the first step to reverse it is to change clothes. Most often, the cold sneaks through your defenses when your clothing gets wet. Snow may melt into your boots, or perhaps you took a bad step when crossing a stream. Perhaps you overheated, or the weather has proven unexpectedly humid (remember, humidity isn't strictly a summer phenomenon) and your base layer got soaked through. Whatever the case may be, change out of your wet gear into something dry before you get too chilled. If your hands are so cold that you're having trouble with fine motor movements, you may want to break out the hand warmers at this point and put on a warmer pair of gloves. Balling your hands up inside your coat pockets helps as well. And of course, do what you can to get out of the wind. Perhaps you lingered for too much time on the summit, took a break for too long without wearing sufficiently insulating layers, or perhaps you're simply not regulating your layers effectively. Whatever the case may be, don't let your condition worsen—reassess your clothing, use hand warmers if necessary, and keep moving to ensure you're generating sufficient body heat.

Eating and drinking something will help as well. Remember, dehydration and hunger exacerbate hypothermia. If you packed a warm drink in a thermos, drink it now. Eat an energy bar or another snack that packs a dense wallop of calories. If you do have a thermos full of warm liquid, placing it inside your clothes can be helpful as well, as you'll absorb some of the heat that it gives off.

If it feels like the situation isn't getting better or some of these options are unavailable, the best course of action is to simply head back to your car as quickly as possible. Again, moving and generating body heat is usually the best way to keep warm. Of course, on a longer camping trip—or if you've become lost—your situation might not be so simple. If you are lost, blindly hiking on without a clear idea where you're going is not a good idea, but you can still generate body heat by moving in place. Jog around the area where you are or start doing jumping jacks or push-ups. After you've generated some heat, you can also crawl into your sleeping bag to retain that warmth, or you might begin searching for a site where you can make camp. You might also stay active by gathering firewood. Starting a fire may not be possible in every situation, but if hypothermia is setting in, it can be lifesaving. You won't need a huge campfire. Even a modest fire will still generate plenty of heat, and is quicker and easier to start when you're working against the clock.

Opposite: Avoiding damp clothing, whether from sweat or moisture in the air, goes a long way in combating hypothermia itself.

Severe Hypothermia

Severe hypothermia is extremely difficult to treat in a wilderness setting, and an introductory guide to winter hiking simply cannot serve as a replacement for expert first-aid training. Thus, the first and best advice for combating severe hypothermia is: don't let it get to that point. Know what to look for, practice an abundance of caution when spending time out on the trail, travel with other experienced hikers and campers, and make sure you're properly prepared, packed, and ready with a backup plan. Even when setting out for a casual, straightforward day hike, make sure you have a map and are familiar with the route you'll be following. If you have a hiking map app on your phone, download the map beforehand. GPS should still work even if you lose cell reception, so as long as you can pull up your map, you should be able to check to ensure you're on the right trail. Always carry extra dry clothes and, if you're venturing many miles from your car, bring any gear you may need in case of an emergency.

If you yourself become afflicted with severe hypothermia, it's likely that you won't even recognize how much danger you're in. Once again, it cannot be emphasized enough that prevention is key when it comes to hypothermia. While this is particularly important if you're hiking alone, it's key to keeping your companions safe as well when hiking in a group. Even with a mild case, someone may act skeptical that they're in danger, particularly if they're inexperienced or unaware of the risk posed. If anyone in your group begins to shiver regularly or show other symptoms, try to get ahead of the situation immediately. Prevention is relatively straightforward, while combating severe hypothermia in the wild can be extremely challenging. You should always take a great deal of care to double-check your gear and group preparedness before setting out for a winter hike, and thus, your standard routine should already serve to mitigate the risk of hypothermia.

Avalanche Basics

Beyond winter storms themselves, avalanches are perhaps the most extreme winter phenomenon that wilderness explorers should be on the lookout for. Fortunately, they are also one of the rarest—at least in most parts of the country. While the threat of an avalanche is a serious consideration in places where there are extremely high-elevation mountains, such as the Rockies and other mountain chains in the western United States, they are incredibly rare on the east coast, where the mountains are significantly lower in height and erosion has created rounder, less severe slopes. According to the National Avalanche Center, the only areas east of the Rockies that see any notable risk of avalanche are the highest, northernmost peaks of the northeast, and even there, the risk is generally very low.

Now, it may be helpful to make a minor point here that will possibly sound like a silly semantics distinction. Nonetheless, it will be helpful when thinking about avalanche preparedness from a broad perspective. Consider that avalanches are typically of much greater concern for skiers than for hikers, for the simple reason that it's difficult (considering what most people think of as "hiking") to head out for a casual day hike in terrain where avalanches frequently occur. There will always be exceptions, of course, but avalanche terrain usually dictates that you'll be snowshoeing, skiing, or even mountaineering in the technical

Avalanches can only occur on mountainsides and cliffs with an extremely steep grade, meaning that winter hikers will only need to watch out for them when hiking in very particular areas.

sense. This, again, is a result of the fact that avalanches almost never occur in the eastern United States except in a few isolated mountain chains in the extreme northeast. In the Rockies and other western mountains, skiers tend to venture to much higher elevations in the mountains in winter than a casual hiker would, and given the seriousness of the dangers posed at such elevations in winter, this is certainly for the best. As we've covered elsewhere, hikers out west should generally stick to well-established, low elevation routes when hiking (or more likely, snow-shoeing and cross-country skiing). Nonetheless, avalanches are difficult to predict, and should you find yourself hiking in avalanche territory without realizing it, it's always worth understanding the basics. The more likely you are to go hiking or skiing in higher altitude areas in winter, the more prepared you should be.

The science of avalanches is complex, and while they're still not perfectly understood, entire books

Avalanche Risk Questions

1. Are you traveling in terrain where avalanches can occur?

2. Is the snowpack unstable? Where might it be unstable?

3. Can I (or others nearby) trigger an avalanche?

have been published on the subject by people who spend their entire lives studying the phenomenon. We can only really cover an overview of avalanche basics here. Avalanche safety falls into the realm of subjects that are best taught by an experienced guide, rather than read about in a book. If you do find yourself regularly exploring in winter in an area with a high risk of avalanches, you'll be better served taking a class or seminar. Make sure everyone in your group at least knows the basics, but again, when adventuring in an area that has a high avalanche risk level, it's better still if everyone in your group has gone through an avalanche safety course.

There are many different types of avalanches, from cascades of loose snow leisurely drifting down a slope, to massive slabs of densely packed snow crashing down a mountain faster than a tractor trailer on the highway. The speed that an avalanche reaches will depend on the size of the mountain (how far the avalanche is able to cascade downhill, building momentum) as well as the degree of the slope. Friction is another major factor: if an avalanche begins well above the tree line on a snow-packed mountain with a steep slope, there will be little to slow its initial progress, allowing it to quickly build up a tremendous amount of momentum. Trees and rocks will of course create friction and thus slow an avalanche down, but once the avalanche has built up enough mass and speed, these obstacles will do little to halt it. Anyone caught in the path of an avalanche will typically find themselves buried deep beneath the snow—an often-deadly outcome.

Three factors must be present for there to be an avalanche—remove one factor and an avalanche cannot form. In order to determine how concerned you should be about encountering an avalanche, ask yourself the following three questions.

1. Are you traveling in terrain where avalanches can occur?
2. Is the snowpack unstable? Where might it be unstable?
3. Can I (or others nearby) trigger an avalanche?

Opposite: Winter storms undoubtedly cause headaches and pose risks, but with these obstacles come fleeting scenes of rare beauty.

Even in highly trafficked areas, like Grand Canyon National Park, winter wildlife is often easy to spot.

8.

WILDLIFE IN WINTER

I f you spend enough time in the wilderness in winter, you will see that this season embodies life just as much as any other. Animals have evolved three basic strategies for surviving winter's rigors: migration, hibernation, and resistance. Some animals may lean partially if not wholly into one strategy, and some—like humans, arguably—utilize a blend of all three.

As a fully converted winter enthusiast, I find spotting rare wildlife in the winter one of the greatest joys of the season. I can watch the barred owls and red-tailed hawks swoop through the meadows of the Hudson Valley near my home. I'll retrace the steps of myriad woodland creatures on a snowy winter day based on the crime scene-like sprawl of tracks over and across a small snowy ravine. I've seen a river otter bobbing up from among the ice patches of a stream in Yellowstone National Park, searching for a site to pull ashore and devour its latest catch. These rare glimpses of incredible creatures in their natural states remind us that the winter landscape is still a vibrant, busy landscape, a place where we might find both calm as well as discomfort, life as well as death.

While hibernation and migration are strongly associated with winter, both adaptations are risky and expensive (in terms of energy and effort). Perhaps surprisingly—at least to a winter-fearing human—many animals survive just fine in the winter without taking such drastic measures. Many, in fact, thrive in the cold and are a thrill to spot on a hike.

Winter Wildlife in Abundance

Though diverse wildlife can be found almost anywhere in the country in winter, the reality is that most wild creatures are even more elusive in winter than during the warm months. A great many animals spend the majority of the winter burrows and

dens. Some hibernate through the winter entirely. In most areas, you probably won't have much trouble spotting squirrels and birds and deer, but the full extent of the wild world tends to get shy once temperatures drop. Not to mention, there just isn't as much wildlife in most areas as there used to be—humans occupy so much space, the wilderness left for animals to roam is patchwork at best. The best opportunities for spotting wildlife are therefore usually in national forest areas, national parks, or smaller but well-managed preserves.

Wildlife havens can be found in all parts of the country, though the best places to spot majestic, rare creatures in a relatively undeveloped environment are generally in the mountainous regions of the continent, such as the more remote regions of the Rocky Mountains. Of course, there's a reason why these areas are largely uninhabited by humans. Some parks are hit so hard by winter, they are essentially (and sometimes literally) off-limits to visitors during the winter months. Glacier National Park, so far north that it shares a border with Waterton Lakes National Park in Canada, receives so much snowfall from September through May that almost all roads through the park close down for the season. While winter wildlife is abundant here—and certainly enjoys the respite from the huge crowds of summer tourists—navigating the backcountry and enduring extreme winter conditions would require extensive coordination and effort well beyond the scope of "hiking."

Still, there are some areas where spotting diverse wildlife in the winter is far easier than you might expect. In places like Yellowstone National Park, you'll find a staggering diversity of creatures roam-ing through the expansive, savanna-like Lamar Valley for the season. Large herd animals like elk and bison generally prefer to settle into valleys like the Lamar for winter, where the mountains provide a buffer from the storms that dump copious amounts of snow in the highlands. To the south of Yellowstone rise the majestic summits of the Grand Tetons, and to their east is another wide, shallow valley where many great herds of elk congregate, shifting back and forth from Yellowstone to the Tetons with the seasons. Some of these herds can easily be observed just outside of Jackson Hole, Wyoming, where they take refuge from the harsh conditions of the high country for much of the winter. In the spring, the herds follow the retreating snows in pursuit of edible grasses, returning north to the Yellowstone National Park region.

Semi-Active Winter Animals

Most warm-blooded animals like mammals and birds are able to remain active throughout the winter, calling upon a variety of techniques and adaptations to resist the cold. Endotherms (warm-blooded animals) must maintain a body temperature that remains well above that of their winter environment, and any animal adapted to a cold region likely packs a serious layer of insulation, whether as fur or feathers. Mammals and birds employ several other strategies for surviving the cold weather, including adding layers of fat for energy and insulation throughout the autumn, huddling, shivering, and fluffing out fur or feathers (remember, pockets of air serve well as insulation).

Huddling is simply when a group of animals con-

Opposite, top: An otter on the hunt crosses an icy creek.
Bottom: The herds of massive bison in Yellowstone National Park are largely unfazed by the cold and snow.

Yellowstone National Park offers views not only of otherworldly landscapes, but of abundant wildlife as well.

gregate together in close proximity for warmth—a snuggle party, essentially. Grouping in this way reduces the amount of exposed surface area for each animal and therefore slows down heat loss. Many small mammals that operate largely independently during the warm months, such as some mice, voles, and shrews, become social in winter and huddle in communal nests to conserve heat. Some birds, such as quail, also huddle at night in winter. Naturally, this strategy explains why you're much less likely to see certain small rodents like mice during the winter, at least out in the wild. (Though this probably isn't the case if you own a barn).

A few animals have developed similar ways to conserve warmth without requiring the body heat of others. Picture the classic image of a fox curled into a ball, with its tail wrapped back toward its own head. Curling up into such a shape helps to reduce surface area and conserve heat. Foxes, coyotes, and wolves all ball up in this manner when cold. Foxes have especially bushy tails, which they are able to wrap like muffs around their heads. Squirrels, which remain partially active during the winter under certain conditions, also have large bushy tails that can help to protect and insulate their back and neck.

Many small mammals live entirely or mostly above the snow, like snowshoe hares, lynx, squirrels, and weasels. As implied by their name, snowshoe hares use their long hind legs like snowshoes to balance on top of the snowpack. The lynx employs a similar strategy, with large feet that help it remain above the snow as it tracks and hunts the wary hare. These creatures stick to climates in the extreme north, however, like the boreal forests of Alaska and Canada.

Smaller mammals, such as squirrels, pine marten, and weasels, weigh so little that they don't risk sinking very deep into the snow in the first place,

Every year, thousands of elk migrate between Yellowstone National Park and the valleys of the Teton range.

and thus are able to remain relatively mobile throughout winter. Squirrels are, of course, famous for stashing their nuts away to survive the cold months. (It's kind of their whole deal). Instead of hibernating, gray squirrels rely on nests of leaves and twigs high up in the branches of trees, sustaining themselves with both fat reserves and stored food. If you've ever walked through the woods when the leaves are off the trees, you've almost certainly seen many squirrel nests. At a glance, it would be easy to assume that these are simply bird nests, as squirrels are not commonly known for their nest building. Nonetheless, in the winter, you will often be able to spot dozens of these nests throughout the tree canopy in a deciduous forest.

Most warm-blooded animals become partially desensitized to cold as they gain greater exposure to it—a lesson perhaps notable for humans who have developed a fear or hatred of the winter, too.

Birds in Winter

While the act of migration is not limited to only birds, migratory birds are certainly the most famous for it. Many birds have adapted to survive the winter by taking their chief evolutionary advantage—flight—and simply leaving until winter has passed. It's estimated that about half of bird species in northern climates migrate south for the winter. Migration itself is a complex subject, and how

A rare short-eared owl scouts a grassy field for prey.

birds manage to reliably follow their migratory routes every year is still not entirely understood. An increasing number of scientists theorize that at least some birds may be able to sense the Earth's magnetic field, navigating by following "guideposts" that are simply invisible to humans. Regardless, the complexities of migration are too great to cover here, especially since most migratory birds won't be observed in the winter months—at least if you live in a northern environment.

Feathers go a long way in insulating a bird against the cold, although this of course depends on the size of the bird, and how specialized its feathers are to this purpose. Unlike many mammals, most birds have a limited ability to modify either themselves or their environment drastically in order to survive the winter. The highly specialized demands of flight, for instance, limit how much fat a bird can pack on for insulation. As a result, many birds must simply remain active and continue consuming calories throughout the winter in order to generate enough body heat. Some birds, primarily small birds, use techniques like shivering to withstand the cold. Just as it does for humans, shivering generates precious body heat through muscle contractions. Larger, more generalist birds like crows and ravens have adapted to their winter environments by shivering continuously throughout the winter when they aren't generating heat through the muscle activity of flight.

One must ponder if this constant need for calories throughout the harshest months of the year might go some way in explaining why crows and ravens are among the smartest animals on the planet, shown to match the intelligence of a seven-year-old human. Corvids have been observed again and again to play in the snow, just like a human child would. Play, of course, burns calories and creates warmth, as does flight. But this need for constant activity through the winter comes with strict caloric demands, and the intelligence of the average corvid certainly must go a long way in ensuring their needs are met.

Naturally, a few bird species are extremely well adapted to the winter. Great horned, barred, and screech owls all do very well in the winter months, and getting the opportunity to observe one of these incredible creatures is one of the finest joys of the winter season.

Discovering Your Region's Unique Wildlife—Bald Eagles and Winter

Few of us are fortunate enough to live close to a park area as bountiful and as beautiful as Yellowstone National Park. But wherever you are, chances are good that winter offers unique wildlife viewing opportunities near your home. All regions of the country have something special about them—something distinct about their ecosystem, some rare flora or fauna. This holds true during every period of the year since many plants and animals only make an appearance during select seasons. Here in the Hudson Valley, one of my favorite seasonal perks is the prevalence of bald eagles along the Hudson River during the winter and spring.

Despite serving as the very avatar of our nation, bald eagles were severely endangered not so long ago. Throughout the early 1900s, their populations declined precipitously due to habitat loss, hunting, and chemical pollution. Fortunately, a

Opposite: Many species of predator birds, like this northern harrier hawk, are much easier to spot in the winter months.

Bald eagles, like other predator birds, are even easier to spot during the winter months.

birds visiting New York's waters from November through April. Nowadays, eagles are easily seen not only along the Hudson, but all around the Mid-Atlantic region, the St. Lawrence Valley, and throughout Connecticut, Massachusetts, and even parts of Vermont and Maine. Bald eagle migration is complex, however, and bald eagles in some parts of the country may even fly north, rather than south. On the Pacific Northwest coast, eagles travel north to follow the movements of salmon. Eagles as far south as California can head all the way to Alaska in search of their preferred food.

Eagles use the same nests year after year, and may even pass these same nests down from generation to generation. Their preference is often a large tree near water with a high open view across the surrounding landscape. Eagles expand their nests every year in preparation for raising the newest generation of hatchlings, and around midwinter, you may sometimes spot eagles carrying sticks and branches back to their nest. This is also a good time of year to try to catch them in the act of a courtship flight, which can be quite a show—the wildest such dances sometimes involve both eagles locking talons and spiraling dramatically toward the ground.

When venturing outside to catch sight of these incredible creatures—or any wild animal, for that matter—remember that the real world is not a zoo, and animals do not exist for our entertainment. This is especially important to remember in winter, being that the season is an incredibly difficult period for any animal. These creatures are busy finding food and rearing their young, and any interruption by a meddling human may cost them a precious meal, or at the very least, will disturb them and cause them to change their perch, wasting precious energy in the process. One caveat to this that's

renewed interest in environmental protections in the 1970s helped pull this incredible bird back from the brink. In the 1970s, it was thought that there may only be a single breeding pair of eagles remaining in all of New York. Today, there are estimated to be around a thousand eagles, with even more thriving in other states throughout the region. Winter, as it happens, is perhaps the best time of year to spot a bald eagle.

Although eagles eat carrion, other birds, and small mammals, their diet is usually predominantly fish-based. Here in the Hudson Valley, this means they tend to nest—and can frequently be seen—swooping over the rivers and parkland of the Hudson River. Indeed, since the Hudson Valley area makes for better winter hunting territory than the colder regions to the north, some bald eagles migrate to the area for the season, with seasonal worth noting is that wild animals generally do not feel as threatened by humans in vehicles as they do by humans on foot (most animals will not "recognize" what a car is, or what it represents), so if possible, try to stay in your car when eagle spotting. Watch through your window, and from a distance of at least several hundred yards, so the eagles can continue their routine in peace.

Whether or not your area is home to grand birds of prey in the winter, the winter season is overall an excellent time of year to practice birding. Since many birds keep warm through the season simply by eating additional calories—and thus, enabling regular movement—you won't lack for birds to observe, even during this quiet time of the year. Additionally, it's far easier to spot most birds in the winter, due to the lack of foliage on the trees. Many excellent guidebooks are available that will help you identify common birds in your area, and this is one of several simple skills you can develop to explore a new hobby and reconnect with nature in a relaxed, engaging way.

Hibernating Animals

The best-known method for surviving the winter is, of course, hibernation. It is far from the most common method, however, as the measures required to hibernate fully through the winter are quite extreme. From the perspective of an ordinary human (much less an insomniac human that struggles to get a good eight hours of sleep in a night) there is undoubtedly something about this survival method that is so unfathomable, so hard to comprehend intuitively, that our imaginations seem inevitably drawn to it. How could anything survive for months at a time simply by sleeping, without any source of sustenance whatsoever?

Many squirrels remain active throughout the winter, depending on conditions, and are a pleasure to observe darting about the quiet cold forest.

The process calls to mind fanciful technologies in science-fiction movies, and yet it is a "technology" that nature managed to perfect millions of years ago. Hibernators pass the winter in a torpid state, meaning they experience a drastic reduction in their metabolism. Biologists group hibernators as deep versus shallow—or, in other words, those which rely on body fat versus those relying on stored food.

Many but not all small mammals are deep hibernators, including bats, ground squirrels, marmots, woodchucks, and some species of mice. The body temperature of these creatures drops to near freezing, their heartbeat slows, and as a result, their blood pressure drops significantly as well. Some small mammals reduce their breathing from one hundred breaths per minute down to four and

A black bear den dug into a steep gully in Yellowstone National Park.

decrease their heartbeat from two hundred and fifty beats per minute to ten. In other words, their body has essentially slowed down to about 4% of its normal operational intensity.

Larger mammals such as bears, badgers, raccoons, and skunks are shallow hibernators, although size is certainly not the only determining factor when it comes to a creature's survival strategy. Some small mammals are shallow hibernators too, like chipmunks. These animals enter a state that is closer to a long, deep sleep than

full-on hibernation, as they occasionally need to rouse in order to feed. While their body temperature remains close to its normal levels, their breathing rate, heart rate, and blood pressure do decrease significantly.

Black bears, perhaps the most famous of shallow hibernators, are able to sleep for months at a time without eating, drinking, or even relieving their bowels, subsisting entirely on body fat built up during the summer and fall. Nestled in their dens, they are able to sleep away the winter sheltered from the elements, even though the dens themselves remain quite cold. In most of the northeast and upper Midwest, black bears inhabit their dens from roughly October until the arrival of spring.

Grizzly bears prepare for their long winter hibernation by eating massive quantities of food in the fall, gaining about three pounds every day leading up to their dormancy period. In order to ensure they've stored up enough energy to hibernate through the winter, grizzly bears need to consume about 20,000 calories per day throughout the busy autumn. As the winter draws near, grizzlies also begin drinking large amounts of water in an effort to flush themselves of waste before hibernation.

Grizzly bears tend to dig dens high up on slopes, carving out a shelter with an entrance that's just large enough for the bear to squeeze through. These small openings close up when the snow begins to fall, and provide good insulation, since the den is only slightly larger than the bear itself. In areas like Montana and Wyoming, temperatures can sometimes drop as low as -60°F in the winter, so every last bit of warmth retained is invaluable.

Hoofed animals with long legs are usually able to move nimbly through all but the deepest snow.

Thriving Throughout Winter

Certain large animals are simply well adapted to surviving and even thriving throughout the winter months. Many hoofed mammals generally do well in the snow, due to their tall, stilt-like legs. This body type allows such creatures to keep the bulk of their mass above the surface of even deep snow, while wading through both snow and water fairly easily. However, due to vulnerabilities inherent in this style of movement—namely thin legs with little to no protection—such animals do best in fresh, soft

snow. Old snow, crusted over with hard sharp ice, can cut their legs, and so will be avoided.

Deer, moose, elk, sheep, and bison tend to herd in places where the snow isn't as deep and movement is easier, such as valleys or small groves. Just like humans, many other animals frequent the same paths between areas, which keeps trails packed down and easier to navigate. Of course, recent heavy snowfall presents just as much of a challenge for even large-hoofed animals as it does for humans. Bison, being less nimble than their deer and elk peers, struggle the most with movement through snow, though their large bodies do help in bulldozing a path.

Bison will continue to forage throughout the winter, undeterred by fresh snowfall.

The most commonly seen large animal through-out much of the country is the common deer. Deer, like most mammals, store extra fat through the summer and fall, and grow a special coat of fur to ward off the cold. This winter undercoat is extremely dense, with oily, hollow hairs that provide exceptional insulation, allowing the creatures to survive in temperatures up to 30°F below zero. While deer do not hibernate, their metabolism does slow down in the winter. When temperatures are fiercely cold, they'll often stay put under shelter for long periods of time — sometimes several days. Deer are browsers, and their diet shifts in winter to accommodate nearly anything they can find. They subsist primarily off of woody browse, which includes the twigs and bark of trees as well as bugs, and you might even catch a deer eating moss or lichen off of rocks.

The Importance of Species Protection—Wolves and Winter

Yellowstone has become famous for its wolf population, as it is one of the few places in the contiguous United States where wolf packs still roam freely. Gray wolves can also be found in some portions of the northern Rocky Mountains, as well as the western Great Lakes region, but the region surrounding Yellowstone has become one of their primary hubs. Wolves are elusive creatures by nature, difficult to spot at any time of the year, but winter at least

Wolves, once extinct in the region, were reintroduced to the greater Yellowstone area in 1995.

makes things a bit simpler. The muted landscape and stark monotones of the snow mean that even a distant gray wolf will stand out as they doggedly pursue their prey. Winter, too, may be the perfect time to glimpse a wolf, because there are few creatures so closely tied to the season in our imagination as the wolf.

Sadly—and somewhat ironically—humanity has always been rather hostile toward wolves, despite the fact that dogs have become our best of friends. While we're happy to make a great deal of effort to curate a good life for our dogs, wolves have been hunted and eradicated just about everywhere they share a habitat with humans. Measures were taken to completely eliminate wolves from many settled areas throughout the late 1800s and early 1900s,

while other predators like bears, cougars, and coyotes were likewise slaughtered in order to protect livestock and more "desirable" wildlife species, like deer and elk. Wolves, which depend upon pack hunting strategies, unfortunately made for somewhat easy targets.

Eventually, however, attitudes toward wild ecosystems began to change. Conservationists and ecologists began to question whether the eradication of wolves was actually beneficial to the environment, even from the perspective of a competing apex predator (us humans). Since the passage of the Endangered Species Act in 1973, the gray wolf has finally begun to receive some help from mankind. Biologists began contemplating the idea of reintroducing wolves to the park and monitoring their effects on the ecosystem. In January 1995, eight wolves were transported from Jasper National Park in Alberta, Canada to Yellowstone. Biologists and ecologists have been closely monitoring the changes occurring in the Yellowstone ecosystem ever since the wolf was reintroduced and have since observed dramatic and often unexpected shifts.

For instance, when the wolf was brought back into the Yellowstone ecosystem in 1995, there was only one beaver colony in the entire park. Two decades later, there are now nine beaver colonies in the park. Such ripple effects in an ecosystem are referred to as a "trophic cascade." Wolves prey on elk, elk eat vegetation, vegetation is also eaten by smaller animals like beavers, and vegetation helps to limit soil erosion as well, which affects waterways, which affects beavers. While wolves and beavers may rarely if ever interact with each other, all aspects of nature are connected, in the end. All aspects of nature—including humans—benefit from a healthy, stable ecosystem. And yes, even the weather and the climate are a player in this complex web. Winters in Yellowstone are becoming warmer and milder, which also softens a bottleneck on the population of browsing animals like elk. With the recent abatement of hard winters, wolves have become the primary agent of elk mortality, stepping in to keep the system in balance when the weather goes too easy on booming populations.

The restoration of the wolf to the greater Yellowstone ecosystem has given scientists the unprecedented opportunity to study what happens when a broken ecosystem becomes whole again. And it has given visitors to the park an opportunity to glimpse one of the most threatened and misunderstood predators in the world today, a creature with a long and deeply intertwined relationship with humanity. In summer, it's nearly impossible to catch a sighting of these elusive predators, but winter makes a sighting far more likely. Wolves are extremely well adapted for the snowy Yellowstone environment, with long legs, well-insulated paws, and wooly coats that mitigate the challenges of the snow. By winter, young wolf pups born in the spring are old enough to join the pack on hunting expeditions, allowing for greater numbers to drive prey into deep snow.

Wildlife Tracks

No matter where you are, learning the basics of animal tracking is an excellent way to begin developing your nature observation skills. Even in a city park, the wanderings of squirrels and raccoons provide ample and interesting material for study. National parks and other large wilderness areas will, of course, offer up even more compelling scenes. Wherever you are or wherever you go, practicing a few basic nature observation skills is a fantastic way to build a deeper intuition and appreciation for a wilderness ecosystem, and helps to mend our damaged attention spans. In the spring and summer, learning tree and mushroom identification skills is an excellent way to develop comfort and familiarity with the woods around you. In the winter, however, it is much easier to focus on the movements of wild animals.

My personal strategy when beginning to learn a new identification skill is to start with a limited set of goals. Even with the ecosystems around us greatly diminished due to human development, there is still so much life and diversity out in the wild. You may initially feel overwhelmed, and that's okay. Even if you focus on a single broad category, like trying to learn all of your local trees, there are likely far more subjects of observation than a novice could hope to memorize in a year. Winter, at least, simplifies things considerably, since so many animals are inactive during the season, or are too difficult to locate to be worth focusing on.

Whether seeking out plants, animals, or fungi, first you must hone in on what species are most commonly found in your area, then learn when they are active. There are many websites and apps today that allow users to tag and identify species at the time they are spotted, which is especially helpful with seasonal beings like birds and mushrooms, which in some cases only appear for a short window of time.

Following animal prints through the snow will tell a fascinating story of wildlife behavior.

This section could easily be expanded into an entire book of its own, and indeed, there are many such books out there that can help you identify animal tracks in any season. If you decide to pursue learning nature observation skills, it's well worth picking up a comprehensive instructive manual. This goes for tracking skills as well as tree identification, birding, mushroom identification, and foraging.

Tracking is the perfect skill to develop throughout the winter. At a time when leaves are crumbled and rotten and herbs and fungi have gone dormant, animal movements are actually much easier to study than at any other time of the year. Winter often creates optimal conditions for the aspiring observer when it comes to following animal footprints and noting other signs. During the summer and fall, the ground will generally be obscured almost entirely by dense growth or fallen leaves. In the winter, however, a smothering blanket of snow will make your task much easier. Often, sets of tracks weave and overlap in a tableau so obvious, you may be able to decipher a wealth of information at a glance.

Like a true detective, a tracker must make deductions based on context clues in the landscape. Do the tracks of one animal intersect with the tracks of others in a way that might suggest a mating couple, offspring, a pack, or even a predator-prey dynamic? Do the tracks suggest that the animal was interacting with the environment around it in a meaningful way, perhaps browsing on twigs or tree bark, or searching for shelter? And finally, can you spot any other animal signs beyond the tracks themselves—droppings, scratchings, shed fur, partially consumed food, or perhaps even a den or nest? Many of these clues will be either subtle or rare, depending on the creature, its habits, its range, and its size.

From here, you'll need to use a bit of imagination. Try putting yourself in the animal's place to figure out why it was acting and moving as it was. Unless you've collected trailcam footage from the scene, you likely won't be able to determine if you're right or wrong, but it's okay to have a bit of fun with your investigative skills, since most likely, there's nothing serious at stake. At least not for you, investigating a wilderness mystery after the fact—assuming that you aren't going about disturbing any animals in their natural environment.

While most types of snow will allow for prints of some kind, especially when tracking larger animals, the best snow for tracking is soft and wet, but not too deep. Such snow will ideally capture a clean print, while still supporting the weight of the creature that made it, without collapsing and ruining the integrity of the track. The morning after a fresh snowfall might seem like the best time to catch such tracks, but keep in mind, animals tend to huddle up in their den or shelter until the snow stops falling. They'll need a chance to get out and about, so realistically, a day or so after a fresh dump of snow may be the most likely time to find tracks.

Opposite: Learning to identify the tracks of various animals in the snow is yet another way to nurture mindful attention and practice observational skills.

9.

A PHILOSOPHY OF WINTER

Even for a lover of winter, it's not all that difficult to understand why so many humans have such an uneasy relationship with the season. Its challenges are fairly undeniable. They are there, they are real, and yet we do have ways to circumvent them. Many of us—at least those of us who spent our childhoods in a wintery environment—have already experienced a time in our lives when we were able to embrace the snow in order to find joy, even in the grasp of winter.

As kids, we seem to intuitively understand how to enjoy ourselves, regardless of circumstances. As children, we embrace the need to play. The wonder is not that so many adults struggle to adjust to winter's harshest challenges. The curious thing to me is that we modern adults seem to have entirely forgotten how to embrace that which is joyful about winter in the first place. We have forgotten how to have fun, how to let our guard down and embrace a thing in spite of its wrinkles, in spite of the mud and cold and discomfort. How is it that children and other animals understand this so easily, and yet as we age into adulthood, we seem determined to convince ourselves that enjoying such things is no longer an option?

There is a video that has circulated around the internet for several years showing a crow in Russia playing in the snow, seemingly inventing the concept of sledding all on its own. From the top of a steeply angled roof, it steps onto a circular bit of plastic, flaps its wings to build up momentum, and proceeds to slide down the roof exactly as one would expect of an experienced snowboarder. As the crow reaches the bottom of the roof, it arrests

Many animals, including the highly intelligent crow, have been observed playing in snow in the winter.

its slide using its wings, picks up the plastic "sled" in its beak, then flies back up to the top of the building, where it proceeds to reenact the experience once again. And again.

The sledding crow's enjoyment is unmistakable. It's having a blast, and it's clearly smart enough to know exactly what it's doing. Nor was this particular crow the only one to ever pull such a stunt: countless crows and ravens have been observed "sledding" and "snowboarding" seemingly just for fun, across multiple continents. Corvids are among the smartest animals on Earth, so none of this should be particularly surprising in that light. A basic intuition for simple physics can help you work out the concept of "sledding in the snow," but just playing around, after all, is something nearly every wild animal has been observed to do. Cats play. Dogs are famous for it. Momma bears can be seen goofing off with their cubs all the time.

In her book *Snow*, the writer and naturalist

Ruth Kirk describes her fascination while observing bears casually enjoy sledding's giddy virtues. "Hiking in the Olympic Mountains . . . I watched a black bear slide down a snow patch on its belly, then lumber back up and repeat the pleasure. In similar fashion polar bear sows stand to catch their cubs at the bottom of a snow slide and wait indulgently while the young run up to slide again. Otters are renowned for their snow slides, and evidently snowshoe hares also play in snow." Wild animals offer a simple yet undeniable reminder that winter playtime can come easily to us—should come easily to us.

Kirk notes that other primates quickly adapt some of the same snow-shaping techniques used by humans, when given the opportunity. Most primate species live in more tropical climates, but a few, like Japanese macaques, exist in regions where snowfall is a regular occurrence. A troop of several hundred macaques were transported from Japan to the primate research center at Beaverton, Oregon. Soon after their arrival at the facility, they began spontaneously fashioning snowballs. Kirk reports: "A male of low status within the troop that winter discovered while eating snow that he could make it into a ball by rolling what he held in his hand along the ground. Intrigued, he pushed and rolled until he had a snowball well over a foot in diameter. Ever since, other monkeys have joined in and now even those who don't make snowballs like to pat them and sit on them." Since then, other Japanese macaques have been observed fashioning snowballs in the wild.

Play is universal, at least among children. Studies looking at a variety of wild animal species have shown that the amount of time animals spend playing during their youth appears to have an impact on their long-term survival and reproductive success. We aren't entirely sure yet how play achieves this, though numerous theories have been put forward. Many biologists have suggested that play is simply a form of exercise, and helps to improve basic fitness. Our studies have shown that play may be important for an animal's learning skills and mental development. The theory goes that, by playing, young animals are essentially conducting experiments with the world around them, manipulating objects and testing out new behaviors. When we play, we learn. We develop. We discover which behaviors work, and which do not. And all the while, we have fun. Fun means: you're on the right track. Play not only teaches us valuable skills but helps us become more psychologically flexible. Our brains, in other words, are opened up to new possibilities when we play.

So why do we lose this instinct when it comes to finding play in the winter?

Winter is hardly the only aspect of our lives that can be challenging to fully embrace. There are very few things in any of our lives that do not offer regular frustrations, after all. There is *nothing* that is constantly and straightforwardly lovable. All seasons of the year have their hindrances and dangers, as well as their aspirational qualities. Our relationships, our friendships, our jobs, our homes, our hobbies—is there anything in our lives that does not at some point draw out stress, worry, or sadness? Why, anyway, is it so much easier for us to look beyond these shortcomings and stressors when we are children? This curious dynamic simply seems to suggest that our hatred of winter is something that we learn, not something that is ingrained within us. It's certainly not something that is necessary.

Cultural attitudes can be terribly difficult to change, to be sure, and perhaps this particular phobia springs from some deeply rooted melancholy that we've been stuck on for a quite a while. Today, however, we have an opportunity to shake it. Hopefully I've shown that embracing the winter is something that is within nearly everyone's grasp. We only need to choose to do so. Perhaps the rest of this book has been enough to convince you that there are ample ways to celebrate the cold, and hopefully I've shown that these attitudes really are not so difficult to change.

When considering the landscape around me, I often force myself to pause and consider: "How could I appreciate this as a painter or a photographer would?" In winter, the environment can sometimes feel so stark that it's as if we are left with little more than an empty canvas. A fresh blanket of white powder coating the earth naturally hides the many nuances that burst out all around us in summer, but even without an inch of snow, even in the midst of a muddy March slump between storms, the world has become essentially monotone. There are browns and grays and apparently little else. Within this monotony, an artist must search for contrasts. Yet when we do find them, we might come to realize that winter has trained us to look more closely. To pay better attention, to embrace both the light and the dark. Contrasts exist all around us, after all, at all times. If we look away, if we try to hide from the darkness and shun the cold, what do we miss?

How can we see clearly, when we focus only on the brightest of scenes and welcome only the easy to love? And what does it do to us, if we never learn to embrace that which is challenging?

Summer is perfectly conducive to a hedonistic, narcissistic worldview, with an open invitation to flaunt our lavish modern lifestyles, our money and

possessions, our friends, and the elaborate parties they throw. Summer allows us to show off our vision of our best self with as few impediments as possible. Summer does not ask us to hide or to hold anything back. Here is the dirty secret to our attitudes regarding winter, in my opinion. We do not hate winter because it is threatening—that's the easy explanation, the answer that sounds just logical enough. There are countless things we love that are dangerous. Countless pursuits we relish, though we literally risk death in the process. Difficulty is rarely ever the thing to turn humanity away. No, we hate winter because we have such a difficult time finding a way to *use* it. We cannot exploit the winter, we cannot hammer it into a shape that serves our needs, and so we do our best to simply avoid it.

Winter gives us far less to brag about, and forces us to confront that which remains, however bleak and unglamorous it may appear. What does it say about us, then—what does it say about our society—that our response to this season is generally no more than anger and depression and withdrawal? If we are only able to experience happiness and pleasure when these feelings come raining down upon us, when we're only able to find joy and contentment in the first and easiest places where we think to look, can we really say that we ever knew anything of happiness and joy in the first place?

To start accepting the winter, to learn its lessons, start by simply ignoring the calendar. It doesn't matter what month it is.

Just find a way to get outside.

Grand Canyon National Park, Arizona

Winter in Grafton Notch State Park, Maine

ACKNOWLEDGMENTS

After writing several traditional hiking guides and one fairly adventurous, country-spanning coffee-table book, it's been an absolute delight to get the chance to work on an experimental hybrid hiking "guide" like this one. If you've picked up this book hoping to learn more about the wilderness in winter, then first and foremost, I would like to thank you for your spirit of curiosity, and for joining me on this unique, potentially challenging adventure.

Putting a book like this together is always a little bit daunting at first, and yet inevitably amazingly enjoyable in the end. The team at Countryman Press has been incredibly helpful and supportive, and I couldn't have made this project happen without everyone there. Many thanks to my wonderful editor Isabel McCarthy for all her hard work on this project—and many others as well, particularly Devorah Backman, Rhina Garcia, Allison Chi, Devon Zahn, and Jess Murphy. Truly, the whole crew at Countryman Press has done really incredible work, and these books would not be possible without their great vision and effort.

Many thanks as well to Dan Crissman, without whom I probably never would have gotten started writing hiking guides in the first place.

Many others have blazed the path before me and helped to steer me on my own hiking journey. Whether they've offered feedback, assistance, companionship on the trail, or have indulged my hyper-specific photography requests (and often all of the above), I want to give my thanks to the following individuals for their help and support in making this book (and my other books!) possible: Todd, Diane, and Danielle Dellinger; Barkley and Bella Dellinger; Debra Krieder; Alicia Kowosky; Evan, Emily, and Ellie Watson; Colin "One L" Talvi; Jonross, Matt, and Kim; Max Pritchard; Lauren Chadwell; Barry Labendz; John Suscovich; Madeline McSherry; Kelsey Schaberg; Lena Deleo; Andrea Ebur; Joe, Pam, and Leah Damour; and most important of all, Imposcar.

And of course, as always, utmost thanks to those who work to preserve and protect our parks and wild lands.

REGIONAL HIKING RECOMMENDATIONS

Northeast

Due to the latitude of the northeast, as well as the fact that most of its mountainous areas are found in the north of this already-northern region, many summits here are home to dangerous extremes of winter weather. New Hampshire's Mount Washington, for instance, holds the world record for the highest measured wind speed not associated with a tornado or tropical cyclone. New York's Adirondack Mountains, as well as numerous mountains in Maine and Vermont, are also subject to intense extremes. As such, the casual hiker is highly advised to stick to easier, low-elevation trails and work up to summiting any high peaks in the winter only after developing the necessary level of experience.

Even in the intense White Mountains of New Hampshire, however, casual hikers can still find numerous options for safer, undemanding trails. In **Crawford Notch State Park**, **Mount Willard** offers some of the finest views in the entire region—with only a 3-mile round trip following a relatively easy trail. To the south, in New Hampshire's lakes region, a hike up **West Rattlesnake** should be accessible to all hikers equipped with the proper gear.

In the Adirondack Mountains of New York, many high peaks are a greater challenge than a casual hiker should accept—but the western and southern Adirondacks are home to much less demanding trails. Novice winter hikers can head to **Bald Mountain**, which features a fire tower, **Rocky Mountain**, which offers incredible views for a 1-mile hike, or **Moxham Mountain**, for those seeking a somewhat longer trek.

Further south, in the Hudson Valley, the **Shawangunk Ridge** is an exceptional area for winter hiking, as many of the trails do not involve significant elevation gain. Many trails in the Catskills will be a challenge in the winter, but hikes like **Giant Ledges** and **Overlook Mountain** are only of moderate difficulty and could be accomplished with the proper gear. Massachusetts, Connecticut, and the southeastern region of New York are still the recipients of harsh New England weather, but are also home to much smaller mountains, and many trails that meander parks with minimal elevation gain or exposure. Thus, finding a casual winter hike in these areas is much less of a hurdle.

Appalachians

Pennsylvania, home to a notoriously rocky stretch of the Appalachian Trail, is also far enough north to see consistent winter weather, though the state is generally hilly more than it is mountainous. Thus, while trails may require careful attention, conditions are rarely too extreme. Many of the state's most popular hiking areas—like **Ricketts Glen**, the **Lehigh Gorge**, and **Council and Lookout Rock**—make for stunning winter hikes but will absolutely require the use of traction gear due to icy trails.

Further south, the weather gets milder, but the mountains also get bigger. In many areas, you'll rarely find snow down in the suburbs, but should nonetheless expect to encounter both snow and ice up in the mountains. This is true along the entire length of the Appalachians, which have their southernmost point in the vicinity of Birmingham, Alabama.

Waterfalls generally make for excellent winter hiking destinations, so long as they are easily accessible. **Crabtree Falls**, in Virginia's **George Washington and Jefferson National Forests**, is no exception. For those willing to tackle a bit of extra mileage, the **Cascades National Recreation Trail to Barney's Wall** makes for an excellent winter hike as well.

Further south, **Great Smoky Mountains National Park**—which falls within both North Carolina and Tennessee—is certainly home to many adventurous treks up towering peaks, but plenty of moderate and easy trails as well. **The Deep Creek Trail** makes for a wonderful option, with a gentle ascent, stunning woods, and beautiful waterfalls. For more falls, hikers can also head to the **Big Creek Trail**, a 5-mile roundtrip hike through dense forest to two different waterfalls.

Midwest

The upper Midwest often endures severe winter weather conditions, particularly near the Great Lakes. However, there are no high elevation mountains in the region, and so trail conditions are often more predictable and more stable than in other northern portions of the country.

At Ohio's Cuyahoga Valley National Park—one of the very few national parks in the northeastern quadrant of the country—hikers will find more than 100 miles of trails, with a variety of terrain and difficulty levels. Both the **Ledges Trail** and the **Brandywine Gorge Trail** are excellent options for a winter outing.

Northern Michigan is home to many great hikes for any season of the year, but a few areas, such as **Sleeping Bear Dunes National Lakeshore**, are even more incredible in winter. Here, hikers can trek along the windswept, frozen dunes, or even snowshoe and cross-country ski on the groomed **Sleeping Bear Heritage Trail** if the snow is deep enough. Further northeast, **Wilderness State Park** offers numerous views of Lake Michigan, and plenty of trails through stately conifers, like the scenic but moderate **Red Pine Trail**.

Minnehaha Regional Park is one of the most popular outdoor destinations in the state of Minnesota, and winter is perhaps one of the best times of the year to visit. Hosting a stunning waterfall, river overlooks, and limestone cliffs, the scenery is even better with snow on the ground.

Wisconsin is home to the 1,200-mile **Ice Age National Scenic Trail**, much of which is ideal for winter hiking—and not just because of the name. The highest point in the state comes in under 2,000 feet, and thus, the majority of hikes in the state do not feature steep, mountainous terrain. **The Lodi Marsh** segment of the Ice Age trail climbs through restored prairie and stands of hardwood and features expansive views of the surrounding countryside. To the north, **Pattison State Park** features a relatively easy trek to several gorgeous waterfalls. At 165 feet, Big Manitou Falls is the state's highest waterfall and the fourth highest east of the Rocky Mountains.

Further west, in a remote and rural region of the Dakotas, **Theodore Roosevelt National Park** gives visitors the opportunity to spot bison, elk, and other wildlife roaming the prairie and floodplains of the snow-covered Badlands. **The Wind Canyon Trail** is a short, accessible, yet scenic starter hike, while the **Caprock Coulee Loop** makes for a more challenging but incredibly beautiful outing any time of the year.

Southwest

Winter may truly be the best time of year to hike in the American southwest. Temperatures are mild, and while all the same winter precautions are as necessary here as elsewhere, at many times conditions may actually be milder than in the summer. Snowfall is typically light and there are fewer visitors, allowing you to enjoy open trails and vistas without battling crowds of other tourists. Indeed, many of the nation's most popular national parks receive only a small fraction of their annual visitorship during the winter months. And out in the wilderness, even a light dusting of snow is enough to transform the southwestern landscape into a place that feels otherworldly, utterly distinct from other regions of the country.

Utah is home to some of the most impressive and unique parks in the nation, though many of them have become over-crowded during the warm weather months. At **Arches National Park**, hikers can more easily navigate the bright desert landscape in the winter to explore popular destinations like Delicate Arch, Double-O Arch, and more. Similarly,

winter is a great time to visit **Zion National Park**, which is home to some truly incredible landscapes. In the winter, however, some popular trails like Angel's Landing may be too dangerous for the casual hiker to attempt, and the park recommends hikers stick to more casual trails, like the **Canyon Overlook trail**, **Emerald Pools**, or for a more ambitious outing, **Observation Point**.

Capitol Reef National Park is more remote than other national parks in the area and is certainly one of the southwest's hidden gems. Featuring bizarre rock formations and incredible textures and colors, a dash of snow over the park only makes the landscape even more striking. **The Hickman Bridge trail** offers hikers great views of an incredible natural bridge, while the **Chimney Rock Loop** is an excellent choice for those who want to tackle a slightly longer and more challenging route.

Arizona, another predominantly desert state, hosts many trails that are ideal for a cold weather outing. **Red Rock Country**, near the popular tourist town of Sedona, is idyllic in the winter, especially if you manage to visit while there's snow on the ground. However, the area remains quite popular on weekends even during the cold weather months. Further north, hikers will find several incredible slot canyons as well as landscapes dotted with unique hoodoos near the small town of Page, Arizona. **Buckskin Gulch**, the **Toadstool Hoodoos**, **Antelope Canyon**, **Horseshoe Bend**, and the **Superstition Mountains** all make for incredible winter destinations.

And of course, **the Grand Canyon** is an absolutely stunning sight in the winter. The crowds are thin, and the summer heat has mercifully relented—here especially, there probably is no better time of year than winter to plan your trip.

West Coast

California is of course a massive state, and like much of the south and southwest, is home to large areas with climates that only rarely see 'true' winter conditions. Yet due to the vast, varied geography of the state, one might easily go from the dry, hot desert to a frigid alpine environment with only a few hours of driving. Indeed, California is home to some of the highest mountains in the country, but casual hikers are advised to stick to the lowlands and foothills.

Death Valley National Park, like other hot and dry desert regions in the southwest, is often best visited in winter. The snow-capped mountains surrounding the valley make for an incredible horizon, and temperatures in this notoriously extreme desert environment will be far more bearable than during the summer months. **The Golden Canyon Trail** offers a short hike to the base of the Red Cathedral rock formation, while an outing to the **Badwater Basin Salt Flats** gives hikers a chance to visit the lowest point in North America—without enduring the scorching, record-setting heat that's usually associated with the area.

Many other popular and well-known California destinations, such as **Joshua Tree National Park**, the **Santa Monica Mountains**, **Angeles National Forest**, and **Big Sur** are excellent destinations for this time of the year. And finally, any park containing majestic redwood trees will be a remarkable sight in the winter.

Hikers seeking something different than the usual mountain vista should set out for the **Cape Falcon trail** in Oregon's **Oswald West State Park**. If you're lucky, you might catch a glimpse a pod of gray whales midway through your hike, as the trail leads to a panoramic outcropping looking out over the Water Bay. Your chances of spotting a whale are best in December and January when they're migrating from the Bering Sea to Baja. Bring a pair of binoculars and be sure to pack the right clothing and gear to ensure that you'll be warm and energized after posting up for an extended period of whale-watching.

To the north, the Olympic Peninsula is home to the only rain forest in the continental United States. The unique landscape and ecosystems of the Olympic Mountains are astonishing any time of the year, but winter nonetheless finds a way to dial up the moodiness. Waterfalls are especially vibrant in this area, given their lush green surroundings, and one of the most beautiful in **Olympic National Park**, Marymere Falls, is located in the popular northern portion of the national park. On the best days, hikers will catch the static beauty of the frozen falls, accompanied by the still-vibrant, teeming woods. Olympic National Park is home to many other incredible trails that make for a great winter hike, but conditions in the region can vary widely in the winter. When in doubt, consult a park ranger before setting out.

Rocky Mountain States

The towering peaks of the Rocky Mountains make this region one of the most stunningly beautiful in the country, but these massive mountains bring correspondingly extreme weather along for the ride. Nonetheless, there are still many trails that meet the criteria for a great casual winter day hike.

In Wyoming, **Yellowstone National Park** is another popular destination that, in many ways, is better experienced in winter than in summer. While most roads through the park close for the season, visitors can still drive through the Lamar Valley all the way to Cooke City. This northern stretch of the park also happens to be the area where large herds of bison and elk roam through the cold weather months, meaning that wildlife spotting is a relatively straightforward matter in the winter. Many short hikes are available throughout the Lamar Valley, like **Wraith Falls** and the **Upper Undine Falls trail**. From **Mammoth Hot Springs**—where the hotel remains open all year round—travelers can even enjoy an easy stroll around the terraces to view the hot springs, though spikes are usually still required.

To the south, in **Grand Teton National Park**, several hikes in the foothills of the mountains are great options for winter. Both the **Jenny Lake Loop Trail** and the **Taggart Lake Trail** offer incredible views of the Tetons, without venturing into dangerous terrain.

Colorado is home to of some of the highest mountains in the country, and these summits obviously pose significant risks to travelers. Even simply navigating the roads through the Rockies in the winter can be a challenging experience. Most hikers, especially those new to winter hiking, should stick to the outer foothills, where low elevation trails nonetheless still host amazing views of the great peaks beyond.

Rocky Mountain National Park offers several easy winter hiking trails, such as the **Sprague Lake Trail** and the **Bear Lake Trail**, where hikers will find tranquil scenery in the landscape surrounding them, and awe-inspiring vistas of the summits beyond, all with very little mileage or elevation gain. Outside of the park, in nearby Boulder, **Chautauqua Park** is home to several easy winter hiking trails, such as the **Chautauqua Trail** and the **Enchanted Mesa Trail**. Both treks provide beautiful views of the nearby mountains without much of a challenge and are easily adaptable into longer hikes.

FURTHER READING

Benyus, Janine M. *The Field Guide to Wildlife Habitats of the Eastern United States* (Touchstone, 1989).

Brown, Vinson. *Reading the Woods: Seeing More in Nature's Familiar Faces* (Stackpole Books, 1969).

Cyancara, Alan M. *Exploring Nature in Winter: A Guide to Activities, Adventures, and Projects for the Winter Naturalist* (Walker & Co, 1992).

Gooley, Tristan. *The Walker's Guide to Outdoor Clues and Signs* (Sceptre, 2014).

Halfpenny, James C., and Roy Douglas Ozanne. *Winter: An Ecological Handbook* (Johnson Books, 1989).

Kirk, Ruth. *Snow* (Morrow Quill Paperbacks, 1977).

Marchand, Peter J. *Life in the Cold: An Introduction to Winter Ecology* (University Press of New England, 1996).

Maurer, Yemaya, and Lucas St. Clair. *AMC Guide to Winter Hiking and Camping: Everything You Need to Plan Your Next Cold-Weather Adventure* (Appalachian Mountain Club Books, 2008).

Roberts, Harry. *Movin' On: Equipment and Techniques for Winter Hikers* (Stone Wall Press, 1977).

Shillington, Ben, and Rebecca Sandiford, *Winter Backpacking: Your Guide to Safe and Warm Winter Camping and Day Trips* (Heliconia Press, 2009).

Stokes, Donald W. *A Guide to Nature in Winter—Northeast and North Central North America* (Little, Brown and Company, 1976).

Various Authors. *Seasonal Guide to the Natural Year*—available for multiple regions (Fulcrum Publishing).

INDEX

Mount Washington in the White Mountains, New Hampshire

ABOUT
THE AUTHOR

Derek Dellinger is a writer and landscape photographer living in the Hudson Valley of New York. He is the author of several books about hiking, most recently *America's Best Day Hikes*. He also writes about food and beverage history, beer, and fermentation. Follow his photography on Instagram @dellingerderek.

Adirondack Mountains, New York